Wethersfield Institute
Proceedings, 1990

THE CATHOLIC WOMAN

The Catholic Woman

Papers Presented at a Conference
Sponsored by the Wethersfield Institute
New York City, September 28, 1990

EDITED, WITH A PREFACE BY
RALPH MCINERNY

IGNATIUS PRESS   SAN FRANCISCO

Cover by Riz Boncan Marsella

With ecclesiastical approval
©1991 Ignatius Press, San Francisco
All rights reserved
ISBN 0-89870-369-7
Library of Congress catalogue number 91-71498
Printed in the United States of America

CONTENTS

RALPH MCINERNY: Preface 7

PRESENTATION OF THE WETHERSFIELD AWARD
to Sheila and John Kippley 9

MARY ROUSSEAU: Pope John Paul II's Teaching
on Women 11

M. JEAN KITCHEL, PH.D.: Pope John Paul II's Teaching
on Women: Some Further Remarks 33

JANET E. SMITH: Feminism, Motherhood, and
the Church 41

MARY ELLEN BORK: Comment on Janet Smith's
"Feminism, Motherhood, and the Church" 67

ALICE VON HILDEBRAND: Edith Stein 73

ANNE ROCHE MUGGERIDGE: Comment on Alice
von Hildebrand's "Edith Stein" 97

MARY HAYDEN: Love: The Center of the
Christian Life 101

LAURA L. GARCIA: Femininity and the Life of Faith .. 125

Ralph McInerny

PREFACE

Women in such countries as the United States are bombarded by views on what it is to be a woman which convey the conviction that, up until the recent raising of consciousness, times have been very dark indeed for the female of the species. A first philosophical entry into the movement was Simone de Beauvoir's *Le deuxiemè sexe*. Betty Friedan's *The Feminine Mystique* brought the issue into the media mainstream of this country. Over the last quarter of a century, the political, legal, and social alterations in the condition of women have been dramatic. Many consider these changes to be an improvement.

It is inevitable that great trends and movements in the wider culture should be felt by members of the Church. There has grown up a tendency to accept the assertions of feminism and to use them as a measure according to which the teachings and practices of the Church are judged. A now disbanded commission of the National Conference of Catholic Bishops produced two drafts of a proposed pastoral letter on women which seemed to exemplify this tendency. On the matter of the status and dignity of women, the Church is put in the dock, from which repentant utterances are expected. Increasingly, the key test of sensitivity to "women's issues" is the question of ordination of women to the priesthood. It is safe to say that most arguments on behalf of this extraordinary suggestion are couched in terms of secular feminism.

There is another, and for Catholics more fruitful, way to regard the relationship between feminism and the Faith. Declarations and demands of feminists can be appraised in the light of the teaching of the Church. This is the way exemplified by the papers and commentaries delivered at the Wethersfield Conference held at the Donnell Library in New York City on Friday, September 28, 1990. Not that this was an occasion devoted to examination and refutation of the secularizing of the question of woman. Rather, it was an occasion when eight remarkable women, adopting the vantage point of the Faith and inspired by the Magisterium of the Catholic Church, as well as such models as Blessed Edith Stein, reflected on what it means to be a woman.

These reflections follow. They do not need my poor praise. Suffice it to say that this was one of the most heavily attended September conferences sponsored by the Wethersfield Institute. The commodious auditorium of the Donnell Library was sold out. The response, during and since the conference, has been overwhelming. It is with great pleasure that I present the papers read at that meeting to a wider audience. May their influence continue to radiate outward to the benefit of all of us, but particularly to all women, both within and outside the Church.

PRESENTATION OF THE WETHERSFIELD AWARD SEPTEMBER 28, 1990

John and Sheila Kippley married in 1963, the year John received his M.A. from the Institute of Lay Theology of the Graduate Theological Union at Berkeley. The previous year Sheila had received her B.S. from the University of California at San Francisco.

Sheila gives as her primary vocation: wife and full-time, at-home mother. Their five children, who arrived in 1964, 1966, 1968, 1972, and 1979, might suggest that this is a necessity rather than a choice, but not so. When John became Director of the Couple to Couple League in 1974, there began a happy coupling of professional and family vocation. Natural Family Planning has found in the Kippleys its most eloquent champions and promoters. They have coauthored articles and books—such as *The Art of Family Planning*, first published in 1975, now in the third printing of its third edition. In season and out, in fertile and infertile period, the Kippleys have spread the good word, earning in the process the gratitude, admiration, and esteem of many.

We shall not list their many contributions and accomplishments—they are written in the book of life, a somewhat more substantial and lasting literary genre than this. In an age of great turmoil in the Church with respect to sexual morality and marriage, there are many things to be done. To defend the teaching of the Church in word and print—and the Kippleys have done this. To refute the arguments of dissenters—and the Kippleys have done this. But nothing drives out the bad like the good, and it is by their steady publicizing of NFP—the method dissenters from *Humanae vitae* refuse to discuss—that

John and Sheila have performed an enormous service to the Church and to their country.

They did not do this for our recognition. Nonetheless, the officers and Board of the Wethersfield Institute are proud to confer this Certificate of Excellence on Sheila and John Kippley.

Mary Rousseau

POPE JOHN PAUL II'S TEACHING ON WOMEN

My thanks to all who had a hand in organizing this conference honoring the Catholic woman, and especially to whoever put me first on the program and then assigned me a topic that simply can't miss. For Pope John Paul II's vision of the dignity and vocation of women is one of the most exciting events of our era. When I look at my materials for this presentation, I am moved to say what Dryden said of Chaucer: "Here is God's plenty!" I'm also grateful for being first today when I look at the names of the women who are to speak after me; believe me, any one of them would have been a tough act to follow.

As to our theme, honoring the Catholic woman, to honor someone is to confer high public esteem upon him. It presupposes the dignity of its recipient; dignity being an excellence that rightly commands esteem. It is right, then, that we begin with Pope John Paul II's vision of the excellence on which we seek to confer our public esteem today. For despite all that has been said recently about women, about human fulfillment and human sexuality and roles in Church and society, there is a fundamental advance in this philosopher-pope's teaching. Indeed, it enables us to dispose at once of any apparent anomaly in the fact that eight Catholic women are speaking today. We might appear to be in the embarrassing position of honoring ourselves. But such is not the case. For the Catholic women who are being honored today are those who truly have the dignity described by the Holy Father. That dignity is not mere birth and maturity as women, coupled with Catholic baptism.

It is nothing less than genuine feminine holiness, a gift which none of us would dare to claim as her own.

The primary source for Pope John Paul II's teaching on women is, of course, his Marian year meditation, the letter *On the Dignity and Vocation of Women* (*DVW*).[1] I propose to interpret its basic theme in the light of other papal and ecclesial writings, notably *Love and Responsibility*,[2] the Lenten talks on Genesis,[3] the encyclical, *The Role of the Christian Family in the Modern World*[4] and the pamphlet deploring the new reproductive technologies, *Respect for Human Life*.[5] The Holy Father affirms the strict equality of women with men in the dignity of being persons. Our equality, in fact, is a religious equality, the deepest equality of all. It is revealed chiefly in two places: the Adam and Eve story in Genesis and the accounts of Jesus' many conversations with women in the Gospels. But our personal dignity is differentiated sexually. And so, equality is not sameness, and difference is not inequality.

Thus we shall begin with the general notion of universal human or personal dignity and then see how that dignity is particularized in the female sex. Once having established the distinctive human dignity of women, we shall make some assessments of the women's movement in our country. For contrary to his bad press, Pope John Paul II has a very good understanding of our American culture. *DVW* applies almost item-by-item to the American feminist agenda. Along the way we shall also see that this celibate male, so widely accused of having no compassion for women, has in fact a compassion for us that is exquisite and deep.

The religious equality of men and women is clear from the creation of Eve as Adam's helpmate, a helpmate precisely in the task of being a person. That task required another person with whom a "unity of the two" might be formed, so that man, precisely as such a unity, might be in the image and likeness of God (*DVW*, pp. 22–25). Adam recognized Eve's religious equality with himself in the joyous cry with which he greeted her, "Bone of my bone and flesh of my flesh!" (Gen 2:23).

Men and women thus have a common dignity and vocation, a kind of fulfillment that is possible only to persons: the *communio personarum*, or communion of persons, that mysterious way in which we can be truly one with each other and still find our individual identities intact and even enhanced. This communion is the theme of almost everything that Pope John Paul II has written or spoken, dating back to his days as a professor of ethics at the University of Lublin. It is, in fact, holiness, our communion with the Divine Communion of Father, Son, and Holy Spirit. It is the grace by which we participate in the inner life of the Trinity. The common call to men and women, then, the dignity of the vocation that we share, is the call to holiness.

Jesus recognized this religious equality in all his encounters with women, where his behavior was startlingly countercultural. Contrary to all the customs and traditions of his time, he spoke to women, in public and about the most serious matters of human life: the identity of the Messiah, resurrection, the meaning of his own death. He was the first to call Jewish women "daughters of Abraham". He made women the primary witnesses of his death and the first to know of, and tell the men about, his Resurrection. Such dignity had never before been accorded to women (*DVW*, pp. 46–60).

This theme of a common human vocation to holiness in a communion with each other that is also a communion with the Divine Communion weaves through the nine chapters of the letter *On the Dignity and Vocation of Women*. Chapter I sets the meditation in the context of the Marian year (I, "Introduction", sections 1 and 2). It is followed by a treatise on Mary, the paradigm of the dignity and vocation of women (II, "Woman-Mother of God", sections 3–5). The next two chapters constitute a Christian sexual anthropology (III, "The Image and Likeness of God", sections 6–8, and IV, "Eve-Mary", sections 9–11). Chapter V, "Jesus Christ" (sections 12–16) is a breathtaking phenomenology of the countercultural behavior of Jesus toward women. Chapter VI ("Motherhood-Virginity", sections 17–22) returns to Mary as the epitome of feminine dignity and the model for all men and women in all interactions and relationships. Chapters VII ("The Church—the Bride of Christ", sections 23–27) and VIII ("The Greatest of These Is Love", sections 28–30) draw important practical conclusions about the roles of women in Church and society. The last chapter (IX, "Conclusion", section 31) is a prayer of thanksgiving to the Holy Trinity as Creator, Redeemer, and Sanctifier of women, for all the "fruits of feminine holiness" throughout the centuries.

We can select from these riches only one or two nuggets. The theme of the communion of persons appears in section 5, "To Serve Means to Reign". Here the Pope describes the psychology of Mary's *fiat*, spoken by one who was both a paradigm and a unique individual woman. God invited her to become the virgin Mother of God. He did not command her, but sought her informed consent. Mary, with her integral freedom, said, "Be it done unto me according to thy word." She thus accepted her individual vocation within the universal human vocation: self-fulfillment in a communion of persons which is also a communion with the Communion of Divine Persons in the Blessed Trinity. She achieved, as Virgin and Mother, the feminine holiness that is the dignity and vocation of women (*DVW*, pp. 14–19).

Many years earlier, as a professor of ethics, Karol Wojtyla had found this communion of persons in his primary philosophical source, the treatise on love in the *Summa Theologiae* of Saint Thomas Aquinas,[6] and made it the thesis of his masterly *Love and Responsibility*,[7] Aquinas offers a simple but profound truth: we humans, who need fulfillment simply because we are limited, needy, deficient, in our very being, can find fulfillment only through union with what is other than ourselves. And that union can come in only one way: through a very special kind of love whose name is *amor amicitiae*. The term, a noun modified by an adjective that has the same root, has no English equivalent. Pope John Paul II calls it "self-giving love" in his letter on women and contrasts it (as does Aquinas) with its opposite, *amor concupiscentiae*, which the Holy Father calls "desire". The first of these is love in the truest sense of the term, genuine or perfect love, in comparison to which desire and all other kinds of love are deficient. For self-giving love constitutes the communion of persons. Desire, on the other hand, does not, and cannot, do so.[8]

To love is, in every case, to wish some good to someone, that is, benevolence. But we can exercise benevolence in two ways, depending on our motivation: we can wish a good to someone, a beloved, for that beloved's sake, or for our own. Thomas Hobbes' example is very enlightening: he once gave money to a beggar, not in order to relieve the poor man's misery, but to relieve his own discomfort and guilt—to feel better about himself, we might say.[9] His love was desire. Although Hobbes wished a good to another, it was his own good that was the center of his concern. Such egocentric love does not unite a lover to the person loved, simply because the focus of concern in such transactions is the self. Desire does not reach out to form a bond with another. It leaves us where we begin, still locked into our original limited being.

Self-giving love, on the other hand, wishing a good to another for that other's sake, does bring about a communion of persons. For when we wish a good to another person for that other person's sake, our love is centered precisely on that other's being, his well-being. In such altruistic loving, we do reach beyond ourselves and extend our own being, for we identify the good of another as our good, too. We thereby possess it as our own. Had Hobbes been concerned first and foremost with the beggar's relief, the good that he would have wished to the beggar would have belonged to Hobbes as well. His union with the beggar, a communion of persons, would have extended his own being, thereby fulfilling his own existential emptiness. Such is the power of love. And such is the nature of human fulfillment, for men and women alike. Our religious equality consists precisely in our ability, and our need, to exercise self-giving love. When we do, we come into communion with each other and with the Divine Communion of Father, Son, and Spirit. "For God is love, and he who lives in love, lives in God, and God lives in him" (1 Jn 4:16).

In section 10, "He Shall Rule over You", Pope John Paul II uses this same distinction between self-giving love and desire to interpret the Adam and Eve story. The first couple misused their precious freedom to reject the dignity of their vocation. They were created as a "unity of the two". But they freely chose desire over love. The penalties of that fateful choice constitute the fallen state into which all of us are born, a state in which, as God said to Eve, "Your desire shall be for your husband, and he shall rule over you" (Gen 3:16). Eve's love for Adam, now desire rather than self-gift, is the refusal of her own dignity as a woman. Adam, dominating Eve rather than loving her, violates not only her dignity and vocation as a woman, but his own dignity and vocation as a man (*DVW*, pp. 33–41).

Taking this story as a paradigm of all human relationships, the Holy Father thus sees the two main ways in which any communion of persons can be ruptured—by desire and by domination. Since these egocentric attitudes are effects of sin, they are meant to be reversed through the process of our redemption. Thanks to the grace of Christ, we can once again become capable of love rather than desire for each other, and of service rather than domination. Our redemption will thus restore, in all interactions among human beings, the communion of persons that is our fulfillment and the glory of God.

This notion of personal fulfillment speaks directly to the basic concern that drives the American feminist agenda. Women's concern for personal fulfillment (what the Holy Father refers to as "self-discovery") (*DVW*, pp. 37–45 and passim) is a deep and legitimate human need. But this legitimate drive is perverted at its roots in feminism by a false view of what personal fulfillment is. The feminist movement is one facet of the individual expressivism deplored by Robert Bellah and his colleagues in *Habits of the Heart*.[10] It is an egocentric urge to desire and dominate other persons instead of finding communion with them in self-giving love. For too many feminists—see, for example, the wife in the film *Kramer vs. Kramer*—freedom translates into the right to be egocentric, to define our fulfillment as we see fit, and to seek it without interference from anyone. If that search means abandoning husband and children, so be it. If it means acquiring power for the sake of power, so be it. If it means sexual license and abortion on demand, so be it. If it means relationships in which we use each other, or calculate devotion to each other's good on the basis of a strict costs/benefits analysis, so be it. First and foremost, we must take care of ourselves. Commitments and relationships are loose and conditional, depending directly on the benefit that we gain for ourselves.

The dynamism of the women's movement of our time is, then, desire rather than self-giving love. The remedy is, of course, simple—but simple does not mean easy. It is the deep conversion that all of us sons of Adam must undergo, the conversion from desire to love, from self-seeking to self-giving, in every interaction with every human being. In Robert Johann's words, "An eros that is sincere . . . discovers that its vocation is to convert itself entirely to liberality."[11] But altruism goes against the grain of wounded human nature. And in our society, there is a special obstacle to that conversion, wrought by the science of psychology and pervasive of our popular culture. With a few notable exceptions (Erik Erikson, for example), psychologists, therapists, counselors, and others regard altruism, devotion, and service to others as masochistic, unhealthy, and harmful to personal fulfillment.[12]

Thus love, love as wishing good to another for that other's sake and thereby coming into a personal communion with him, is not even understood in our culture. One of the major tasks of enculturating the papal vision of the dignity and vocation of women is to correct this truly basic misconception. For there are three counts on which self-giving love is not masochistic. The first (and deepest) we have already seen: the very communion of persons that such love generates. There is an unavoidable existential fulfillment for the giver of love, one built right into the very structure of love. Thus there is no possibility that self-giving love might lead to self-destruction or self-abasement. It always brings us into communion with the three Divine Persons.

But there are two other ways in which self-giving love leads to fulfillment rather than destruction. Love, after all, involves giving to others not just gifts and words and time and energy, but giving our very selves. But the giving of oneself presupposes having a self to give. And so, the love that builds a communion of persons absolutely requires the personal development of its giver. Thus the Holy Father's call to women to accept the vocation of self-giving love is also a call for women's self-development, a recognition of our rights to education and employment, to the discovery and use of our talents, to positions of influence and power, to care for our health and safety. The only requirement is that our self-development must have its right orientation—not self-fulfillment for the sake of the self, but self-development in order to have something to give.

And finally, self-giving love is anything but masochistic in its hope for reciprocity, the hope that those whom we love will love us in return. The operative word here is *hope*. Desire demands the return of love as a condition of its giving. Genuine love hopes for reciprocity without making it a condition or demand. For after all, if love is the wishing of a good to someone, and the greatest good we can wish to anyone is his or her fulfillment as a person, then we must want those we love to exercise love in their turn. And to whom might their love be directed? Why not to the one who, by loving them first, enables them to love in return? Reciprocity, far from spoiling a communion of persons, redoubles it.[13]

Such, then, is the religious equality of men and women in the dignity of our common vocation, the holiness by which we enter into the very life of God. How is this general human dignity differentiated in the two sexes, so that women enjoy a distinctly feminine dignity? Here we must look to the Holy Father's phenomenology of that action in which sexual differences are dramatically clear and undeniable—the act of sexual intercourse. When that act is what it is meant to be, it is "a great sacrament" in reference to Christ and the Church. It is then rightly called the act of *making* love.

A student once remarked, on learning that impotence is an impediment to marriage and that unconsummated marriages can be dissolved, "Gosh, I never thought the Church would put so much emphasis on sex." In the works of Pope John Paul II, we see an emphasis that is quite new and even more startling (until we understand it). His view of the act of making love is the keystone of his entire sexual ethic, his family ethic, his views on women, and his understanding of the Eucharist and the sacramental priesthood. He sees in the simultaneous orgasm of loving spouses a uniquely intense moment of the communion of persons. And in that action, he sees not only the epitome of married love, but a kind of model of what all of human life should be—ecstatic and passionate reciprocal self-abandon.[14]

The differences revealed in the act of making love are not the stereotypes, so rightly hated by feminists, of male strength and control and female weakness and passivity. But stereotypes are not invented out of thin air. They have their roots in human experience, experience that somehow becomes distorted and caricatured. Thus, men and women, as the act of making love shows, are not rivals in a power struggle, but partners—complementary partners—in a joint urge for self-abandon that makes them putty in each other's hands. Orgasm is a high point of reciprocal self-giving love. But the self-giving is different for the two spouses, different in ways that are not trivial and that cannot be overlooked. The chief difference is in male initiative and female receptivity. For the sex act even to seem to happen, a husband must act, in an energetic and obvious way, and his wife must receive his action. He exercises a kind of initiative, and she is receptive to it. But his initiative is not aggressive and oppressive. It is a headlong rush to hand himself over to his woman, lock, stock, and barrel. And her receptivity is not passive and degrading. She gratefully accepts his compliment and responds with an equally active gift in kind, rushing to hand herself over to him, lock, stock, and barrel.

For a brief moment, then, the two become putty in each other's hands, achieving a communion of persons that is uniquely intense for both of them. That uniquely intense moment is sacramental. As a sacrament, a causal symbol of their entire life together, their communion carries over, from the bedroom to the kitchen, the living room, the yard—wherever they go as they live out the promise of that moment.[15] Their special moment is also sacramental for the rest of mankind, a model for all other interactions of all human persons—in family life and business, education, health care, politics, and international relations. This momentary marital holiness is meant to characterize all of human life. For holiness is nothing more, and nothing less, than our sexually differentiated exchange of self-giving love in all of life, in ways that are appropriate to each encounter with other men, women, and children.[16]

There are, then, genuine differences between the sexes that are natural, not just cultural, and sexual, not just individual differences that might be found in people of either sex. They are differences in perceiving, judging, and choosing; differences in the exercise of self-giving love; differences for forming communions of persons.[17] They are differences in holiness and thus in personal dignity. The Holy Father thus provides a crucial element for understanding women that has been missing from the public discussion in this country: an understanding of human sexuality that neither denies nor overemphasizes the differentiation of human beings into two kinds, masculine and feminine. By taking human nature to be analogous in men and women, he shows our absolute equality with each other as persons. And yet, he gives full value to *la différence*, so that sex, an obvious bodily difference, is not split off from personhood but is pervasive of it.[18] Thus, equality does not mean sameness, and difference does not mean inequality. He avoids the dilemma of either treating men and women exactly alike or else making one sex inferior to the other. Thanks to this analogy, he offers a rich and attractive view of women's dignity that takes advantage of our special traits as women, and yet sets us side by side with men in a joint, complementary search for human fulfillment that is as differentiated as people are. *Vive la différence!*

In his talks on Genesis, Pope John Paul II invented a wonderful phrase for human sexuality, "the nuptial meaning of the body". He means not just the male and female genital organs as they function in the sexual act, but a feature of the entire person of every man, woman, and child. Sexuality is, of course, much more than a mode of reproduction. But it is that, and that basic biological differentiation pervades our personalities and affects everything we think and do and say. Thus, in every human encounter, something resembling the nuptial union must occur. For our bodies bear a meaning that is always there, to be expressed or violated, as we freely choose either to desire or to love the people we meet in daily life. All human interactions, even buying a paper at a newsstand, must be characterized by self-giving love that has a nuptial character, that is marked by a fidelity and permanence appropriate to the occasion, by sexual differentiation, and by some sort of fruitfulness for new human life.

The Church's emphasis on sex, then, is well placed. For the great majority of the world's people, marriage and family life are the way to salvation. Even celibate people are born into families, and the quality of a family's life as a communion of persons depends directly on the quality of the sexual intimacy of the parents. What is the reason for the power, the sacramental power, of lovemaking? One reason is the unique nature of orgasm as an experience in which we are drawn out of ourselves, our attention and concern at least momentarily decentered from our fascinating egos. Any exercise of self-giving love requires that we focus attention and concern on the one we love. Regular marital orgasm builds the habit—the habit otherwise known as the virtue of charity.

But further, in order really to say a deep and heartfelt *fiat* to our vocation to self-giving love, we have to believe, in our bones, in the reality of love. This basic credibility of human love is not given to us at birth, nor even at baptism. We have to learn that love is real before we can begin to believe that it is the supremely real entity of our world; that God is Love. The conviction that love is real comes to us exactly as does our conviction of the reality of anything else—through our five senses. "How can they love God, whom they do not see," asks Saint John, "if they do not love their neighbor whom they do see?" (1 John 4:21). But before we can love, we must be loved, and know that we are loved, in some sort of sensory experience.[19] Now the act of sexual intercourse is the most intense experience of the most intense of our senses, the sense of touch. Thus, sacramental spouses know, in their bones, that love is real. They feel that reality, in the very same moment in which they are drawn out of themselves and toward each other by the overwhelming pleasure of making love. Truly, such a seduction could only have been invented by a wisdom that is divine.

The Holy Father's context here is Aquinas' unique view of the body-soul makeup of the human person. Midway between a gnostic spiritualism and a crass materialism, Aquinas offers a third view, namely, that both matter and spirit, mind and body, are essential components of the human person, united so closely as to constitute a single substance or entity. For Aquinas, a man is an incarnate spirit or a rational animal.[20] This notion of the unity of the human person is crucial for understanding sexuality. For our sexual identities are central to our identities as persons. My being female, for example, is not on a par with my green eyes, my ability to teach philosophy, or other hereditary traits that I could lose without ceasing to be myself. If, at the moment of my delivery, the doctor had said, "It's a boy!" he would not have been announcing *my* birth. A child of the other sex would have been someone else, not I. Sexual differences, revealing the nuptial meaning of our bodies, are important to all that we think and do and say, even for those of us who never make love or never reproduce.[21]

The nuptial meaning of the female body is a certain "primacy in loving" that is due to our having bodies that are apt for conceiving, bearing, delivering, and nursing babies (*DVW*, pp. 61–70 and 96–102). This primacy is not, of course, the stereotypical magic of women's intuition, that supposedly mysterious gift by which we can read minds and achieve intimacy without the hard work of honest communication. But we do have a special sensitivity to persons and their needs, thanks to our having bodies that are apt for the physical closeness to another person that occurs in conception and pregnancy. Mothers are often the first to notice their children's psychological needs, for example, and wives perceive their husband's mood changes before their husbands do. That sensitivity can flower whenever persons are entrusted to us, beginning with the crucial first stage of development when all of us are entrusted to our mothers for nine months *in utero*. Women enjoy an incipient psychological closeness to persons, in all situations, that is rooted in our capacity for the physical closeness of pregnancy. The dignity of women, then, is located in our distinctively feminine, spousal, and maternal capacity to foster new life in other persons. With that innate, sensitive maternal insight into their individuality, we often know by a kind of instinct how to nurture their ability to love.[22]

This nuptial meaning of the feminine body, our capacity to nourish human life in a myriad of ways, also speaks to the agenda of feminism. Far from condemning us to a degrading and dull domesticity, this notion of feminine fulfillment opens wide vistas. Women's realities and women's choices are—or should be—as varied as are the modes of feminine loving. Thus we can find the dignity of our vocation, our feminine fulfillment, in any role or any action in which we can exercise our sensitive and intuitive self-giving love. One highly dignified life is that of a full-time, stay-at-home wife and mother. Domesticity, which consists in cultivating a genuine marital intimacy and in teaching children how to love in their various sexual and individual ways, is one of the most creative and demanding challenges that anyone could ask for. Other possibilities would be a single life, a widowed life, a life of vowed virginity, a sterile marriage, a life as an active or contemplative religious, a life combining career and family, a life on an invalid's bed or in a wheelchair. To feminists seeking wider roles and opportunities for women, the Holy Father's vision offers a strong basic principle: whatever women are physically and psychologically capable of doing as an enactment of self-giving love is a legitimate occasion of the dignity and vocation of women. Thus all roles in Church and society that women can lovingly fulfill ought to be open to us.[23]

This principle brings us, of course, to the flash point of feminist anger against the Pope—his insistence that the ordained priesthood be open only to men. It is no accident that women's ordination is such a flash point, because it is the focus of clashing views on human sexuality. For those who insist on absolutely everything being open to women, sexuality has no personal importance. It is relegated to a mere physical attribute that is significant only for reproduction. But for the Holy Father, sexuality is not just central to what we are as persons. It is also central to the sacramental life of the Church, especially at the point where three sacraments—matrimony, Eucharist, and orders—come together to provide the grace by which human communions of persons are drawn into the Communion of Father, Son and Spirit in the Trinity. The need for a male priest as a requirement for the sacramental symbol of the Eucharist, brings us back to the act in which the differentiation of the sexes matters the most and is dramatically evident—to the human marital act, the act of "making love". Here is the "great sacrament in reference to Christ and the Church". Male initiative and female receptivity are especially important in the Eucharist, in which the priest reenacts the marital love of Christ the Bridegroom for his Bride, the Church. In the Eucharist, the Divine Bridegroom gives himself up for his Bride and becomes one flesh with her. Thus, matrimony, the "great sacrament" of which Saint Paul speaks in Ephesians (5:32), while it does represent and effectively cause the presence of Christ for husband and wife, is but a faint and distant image of that divine marital act.

In this most marital of all marital acts, the initiative is entirely with the Divine Bridegroom, who "first loved us while we were yet sinners" (1 Jn 4:19). That love is received then, by the free, grateful receptivity of the human persons who are the collective Bride, as we respond by our gift of ourselves to Christ, "giving up our bodies as a living sacrifice, holy and acceptable to God" (Rom 12:1). This divine marital love, in which the Son of God makes himself putty in the hands of sinners needing redemption, is the heart of the sacrifice of the Eucharist. Its counterpart is our acceptance of that gift, by which we make ourselves putty in the hands of Divine Love.

The sacramental symbolism of bride and bridegroom in the Eucharist is no small matter, for our sacraments are not just symbols. They are symbols that cause what they signify, cause it precisely by signifying it. Thus the accuracy of the symbols is all-important. The pouring out of divine marital love in the Eucharist, then, requires that the human symbol—the visible, audible, tangible enactment of that outpouring of divine love—be accurate and clear. Otherwise, it will not effectively cause or realize that love, the love of the Divine Bridegroom for his Bride.

We have not lost the principle that all roles and actions which women are physically and psychologically capable of performing should be open to us. But that principle has to be coupled with the sacramental nature of human sexuality. For the priest, as "another Christ", must be able to re-present, in what he is as a person, the initiating love of the Son of God who is also the son of Mary. He must, in other words, be a "he", not a "she". His body must have a masculine nuptial meaning. He must have male perceptions and judgments, male love, male personal identity. A woman cannot, by reason of her physical and psychological makeup, stand in the place of the Bridegroom in the Eucharist, any more than a wife can exchange roles with her husband in the act of making love.

The question of women's ordination is not, then, a question of equality, of justice or rights, or of roles in a social organization. It is a question of what is and what is not ontologically possible, given the sacramental symbolism of human lovemaking and of the Eucharist. Were a woman to play the role of the priest in the Eucharist—and role-playing is all that she could do—the effective power of the sacramental symbols would fail. Words would be spoken, gestures performed, but nothing real would happen.[24]

Jesus' selection of male apostles to be his priests was not, then, a culture-bound, sexist act but a fully enlightened choice that suited his sacramental purpose (*DVW*, pp. 87-90). His establishment of a male priesthood was no denigration of women. We are still the religious equals of men, equally dignified, equally beloved as persons, equally capable, with our feminine primacy in loving, of the holiness to which all of us, men and women, are called. In fact, holy married women are models for priests in their search for holiness as celibate men.

The analogy between religiously equal male and female persons casts light on other feminist demands for equality with men in social, economic, and political life as well as in ecclesial roles other than the ordained priesthood. For religion, in the Holy Father's thought, is not just one area of human life among others; it is the basis of economic, political, social, and ecclesial life. All of human life, all of human action, is meant to bring us into communion with each other so that we might thereby enjoy communion with the Blessed Trinity. Thus all of human life is religious and must be governed by the laws of love. There is no room for the slightest sexist discrimination anywhere in human life. But the equality of men and women is an analogous one, so that the differentiation of the sexes must not be lost, not in any of our behavior, any of our laws, any of our customs and traditions. The primacy in loving that is central to our dignity and vocation as women must be treasured, developed, and institutionalized. Our laws, then, must somehow allow for the difference between the sexes, and the ERA demanded by the feminists would have been a tragic mistake. To give only one example, women need laws providing special help when they are left to cope alone with the difficult situations that men and women create together. The Holy Father's heart goes out to such women, those trapped in the poverty of single parenthood or in the psychological aftermath of abortions, for example (*DVW*, pp. 53-55). We might question, on the same basis, laws that would place young children into daycare so that their mothers might work away from home. It might be better for the dignity and vocation of abandoned or widowed mothers if they were paid to stay home and care for their children.

The Holy Father's letter returns at the end to Mary as the epitome of feminine holiness and model for all persons of both sexes. What is decisive for her dignity and vocation is decisive for us all. As equal persons, men and women alike are called to communion with the triune God, in and through our communion with each other. Throughout the Bible, from Eve to the woman of Revelation 12, feminine receptivity shows men the way to communion with God. For before God we are all receptive, all passive to the initiative which brings us his love and calls us to make a return in kind, with our own "Be it done unto me according to thy word."

Pope John Paul II ends his meditation with two fervent prayers. The first is a prayer of thanks, on behalf of the entire Church—thanks to God for the gift of women, for the Incarnation and other great deeds of feminine holiness throughout the centuries. The second is a prayer to Mary, that she will obtain for all other women the grace of finding the dignity of their vocation, the vocation to love.

It seems appropriate, since we are gathered here in the heart of Manhattan, to end these considerations with an item from *The New Yorker* magazine, dated April 23, 1990. It is a poem about that human experience on which the Holy Father's teaching on women finally rests, the sacramental lovemaking of Christian spouses. The poem, written by Mary Stewart Hammond, speaks of male initiative that is anything but aggressive or oppressive, and of female receptivity which is anything but passive or degrading. It speaks as well of death, and resurrection, and even of ascension. Its title is "Making Breakfast".

> There's this ritual, like a charm,
> Southern women do after their men
> make love to them in the morning.
> We rush to the kitchen. As if possessed.
> Make one of those big breakfasts
> from the old days. To say thank you.
> When we know we shouldn't. Understanding
> the act smacks of Massa, looks shuffly as
> all getout, adds to his belly, which is bad
> for his back, and will probably give him
> cancer, cardiac arrest, and a stroke. So,
> you do have to wonder these days as you
> get out the fatback, knead the dough,
> adjust the flame for a slow boil,
> flick water on the cast-iron skillet
> to check if it's ready and the kitchen
> gets steamy and close and smelling
> to high heaven, if this isn't an act
> of aggressive hostility and/or a symptom
> of regressed tractability. Although
> on the days we don't I am careful
> about broiling his meats instead of
> deep-fat frying them for a couple of hours,
> dipped in flour, serving them smothered
> in cream gravy made from the drippings,
> and, in fact, I won't ever do
> that anymore period, no matter what
> he does to deserve it, and, besides, we are
> going on eighteen years, so it's not as if we
> eat breakfast as often as we used to,
> and when we do I now should serve him
> oatmeal after? But if this drive harkens
> to days when death, like woolly mammoths
> and Visigoth hordes and rebellious kinsmen,
> waited outside us, then it's healthy, if

primitive, to cook Southern. Consider it
an extra precaution. I look at his face,
that weak-kneed, that buffalo-eyed,
Samson-after-his-haircut face, all of him
burnished with grits and sausage
and fried apples and biscuits and my
power, and adrift outside himself,
and the sight makes me feel all over
again like what I thank him for
except bigger, slower, lasting, as if,
hog-tied, the hunk of him were risen
with the splotchy butterfly on my chest,
which, contrary to medical opinion, does not
fade but lifts off into the atmosphere,
coupling, going on ahead.[25]

NOTES

[1] Pope John Paul II, *On the Dignity and Vocation of Women* (Boston: Daughters of St. Paul, 1988). Hereafter cited in the text as *DVW*, with page numbers following.

[2] Karol Wojtyla (Pope John Paul II), *Love and Responsibility*, trans. by H. T. Willets (New York: Farrar, Straus & Giroux, 1981).

[3] See Mary G. Durkin's summary of these 56 weekly addresses, *Feast of Love: Pope John Paul II on Human Intimacy* (Chicago: Loyola University Press, 1983).

[4] Pope John Paul II, *The Role of the Christian Family in the Modern World* (Boston: Daughters of St. Paul, 1981).

[5] Joseph Cardinal Ratzinger, *Instruction on Respect for Human Life in Its Origin and on the Dignity of Procreation* (Boston: Daughters of St. Paul, 1987).

[6] The questions on love are in the *Summa Theologiae*, I–II, 26–28. For an excellent exposition of their doctrine, see Robert Johann, S.J., *The Meaning of Love* (Glen Rock, N.J.: Paulist Press, 1966).

[7] See note 2, above.

[8] Both terms are problematic in English. Self-giving love, as we shall see, has false connotations of masochism. And desire refers to many legitimate affections as well as the possessive domination or use that the Holy Father has in mind.

[9] This story, which Hobbes tells on himself, is reported in *John Aubrey's Brief Lives*, ed. Oliver Lawson Dick (London: Secker and Warburg, 1949), p. 157.

[10] Robert Bellah, *Habits of the Heart* (Berkeley: University of California Press, 1985).

[11] Johann, *The Meaning of Love*, p. 78.

[12] See the fine assessment by Paul C. Vitz, *Psychology as Religion: The Cult of Self-Worship* (Grand Rapids: Eerdmans, 1977).

[13] See Saint Thomas Aquinas on the "mutual indwelling" of lover and beloved, *Summa Theologiae*, I–II, 28, 3.

[14] See "Marriage and Marital Intercourse" in Wojtyla, *Love and Responsibility*, pp. 270–78. Here Professor Wojtyla recommends to Christian spouses an effort to achieve simultaneous orgasm and even the use of a sex therapist, should such help be needed, for this orgasmic communion of persons is the heart of the sacrament of matrimony.

[15] See *Embodied in Love* (New York: Crossroad Press, 1983), co-authored with C. A. Gallagher, S.J.; George A. Maloney, S.J., and Paul F. Wilczak.

[16] The contagion of love, through its credibility in loving spouses, is one of the important themes of *The Role of the Christian Family in the Modern World*. John Paul II expects the love of sacramental spouses to spread to the entire world, thus creating a "civilization of love".

[17] For a modest attempt to identify some natural sexual differences, see my "Abortion and Intimacy", *America* 140, 20 (May 26, 1979), pp. 429–32.

[18] See *DVW*, pp. 33–41 and 79–92, and my article "Pope John Paul II's *Letter on the Dignity and Vocation of Women*" in *Communio International Catholic Review* XVI, 2 (Summer 1989), pp. 220–26.

[19] For a brief and readable account of how the sense of the reality of love grows throughout the stages of the life cycle, see Rev. David P. O'Neill, *About Loving* (Dayton, Oh.: Geo A. Pflaum, Publisher, Inc., 1967). O'Neill parallels Erik Erikson's view of the eight stages of life with passages from the Bible and with wonderfully apt photographs.

[20] For an integral philosophical and theological Thomistic view of the human person, see Jean Mouroux, *The Meaning of Man* (Garden City: Doubleday and Co., Inc., 1961).

[21] For a striking study of the nuptial meaning of Jesus' body as seen by Christian painters of the Renaissance, see Leo Steinberg, *The Sexuality of Christ in Renaissance Art and in Modern Oblivion* (New York: Pantheon Books, 1983).

[22] See my article "Pope John Paul's *Letter*", pp. 219–21.

[23] See my "The Roots of Liberation", *Communio International Review* VII, 3 (Fall, 1981), pp. 250–76.

[24] The basic principles of this sacramental theology were set forth in two articles by Donald J. Keefe, S.J.: "Biblical Symbolism and the Morality of *in vitro* Fertilization", in *Theology Digest* 1974, pp. 308–23; and "Sacramental Sexuality and the Ordination of Women", *Communio International Catholic Review* V, 3 (Fall, 1978), pp. 228–51. Philosophical support for Keefe's views can be found in my "The Ordination of Women: A Philosopher's Viewpoint", *The Way* 21, 3 (July, 1981), pp. 211–24. Sister Sara Butler, M.S.B.T., once a prominent supporter of women's ordination, now sees Aquinas' anthropology as central to the question, and calls for a sympathetic reading of the Vatican's 1977 "Declaration on the Question of the Admission of Women to the Ministerial Priesthood". See her "Second Thoughts on Ordaining Women", *Worship* 63, 2 (March, 1989), pp. 157–64.

[25] Mary Stewart Hammond, "Making Breakfast", *The New Yorker*, April 23, 1990, p. 40.

M. JEAN KITCHEL, PH.D.

POPE JOHN PAUL II'S TEACHING ON WOMEN: SOME FURTHER REMARKS

In my role as commentator on Mary Rousseau's excellent paper, I wish to focus on the single issue which for me dominated the paper no matter how I approached it. Through focus on that one issue, I shall try to draw attention to certain points in the paper which I believe deserve our especially thoughtful contemplation. The issue I have chosen is the importance of unconditional self-giving love to universal human dignity and therefore to the dignity of women.

Philosopher that I am, two passages from sacred Scripture came immediately and persistently to my mind as I read the various drafts of Rousseau's paper.

When Saint Paul wrote his letters to the Christian community at Corinth, he wrote to Christians immersed—much as we are—in a society in which the perversion of authentic human love into mere desire was rampant. The admonitory lines of his hymn to love, used so frequently in the celebration of Christian marriage, are familiar to us all: "If I speak in the tongues of men and of angels, but have not love, I am a noisy gong or a clanging cymbal" (1 Cor 13:1). In this passage and in the entire hymn, Saint Paul reminds the Corinthians and us that it is love which calls us to and achieves our authenticity. Without love we do not embody what it means to be fully human.

As Pope John Paul II has so frequently pointed out, we are constituted by nature as beings meant to love, meant for love. In his prepapal writings,[1] Wojtyla develops a difficult philosophical anthropology that is both incarnational and phenomenological. For him, the human person is a conscious being self-constituted by conscious acts which are free, self-determining, and ordered to the true good. The personal self relates to itself as both subject and object; it is autoteleological—that is, it has the constitution of itself as a proper end of its own actions, it is its own, though not its final, end.

These are really only philosophical ways of speaking about what everyone recognizes as love—the conscious choosing of a valued goal, the rational appetite for a good. What is important is that the appetite be rightly ordered to the proper good, and Wojtyla's picture of man points to a great pitfall: man can easily be confused into the belief that he is not only a proper end for his self-constituting actions, but also that he, through his actions, is his own final end. It is to such a confusion that the third and fourth chapters of *Mulieris dignitatem* (On the Dignity and Vocation of Women) speak when they examine Genesis' revelation of the relationship between God and man. Genesis tells first of the "unity of the two" which characterized Adam and Eve, each an "I", the subject of a personal inner life. And then it tells of the disunity sown between the two when they, together, disordered their love from its proper good by disobeying the only restrictive commandment which God had given them.

The second passage of Scripture which came to my mind is Saint Matthew's Gospel (22:36–38) when Jesus is asked to name the greatest commandment of the law. His reply is well-known: " 'You shall love the Lord your God with your whole heart, with your whole soul, and with all your mind.' This is the greatest and first commandment. The second is like it: 'You shall love your neighbor as yourself.' " The command to love expressed here is actually threefold: first and foremost to love God; to love one's neighbor; but also—and this is often overlooked or misunderstood—to love oneself. The fulfillment of these commands is, as the letter on the dignity of woman shows us, constitutive of our human nature and our human dignity, but what does this fulfillment entail?

In order to love a being, one must apprehend it as good, which in turn implies some authentic knowledge of the being in its nature. Therefore, as we learn from Genesis, God revealed his goodness through the material creation especially to man, whom he had created in his own image, so that man, apprehending the revealed goodness might freely love the Good as the Good had loved him. God made himself knowable and made us able to know him. He did this without condition and without any merit of our own. Never in the ensuing drama of man's fall and salvation does God condition or withdraw his love. It endures, as *Mulieris dignitatem* notes, more surely than the love of mother for child (III, no. 8). Finally, God made himself known in the very Incarnation by which man would be redeemed from the penalty of his own disordered love.

The way in which the first parents rejected the goodness of God is also important to the teaching of *Mulieris dignitatem*. Adam and Eve rejected God's goodness as imaged in their human nature. Tempted by the Evil One to re-create their nature through disobedience to God's will for them, they lost its pristine goodness. They lost the radiance, order, and integrity by which human nature was indeed the *imago Dei*, thereby losing the goodness they were meant to love in themselves and in one another. To translate this into the terms of the Pope's philosophy: as objects of love, they became less truly appealing to the rational appetite; as subjects of love, they became less well-disposed to the truly good. Or, in the language to which Dr. Rousseau has drawn our attention in the papal letter, self-giving love was displaced by desire, in part because the now diminished self was no longer as worthy a gift and no longer truly lovable, only desirable in the way of other things. The communion of persons was displaced by domination and subjugation, the relationship man naturally holds toward things. No longer could Adam and Eve see clearly what it means to be persons made in the image and likeness of God, and no longer could they love in the image and likeness of God's unconditional love.

It is with this same clouded vision that we try to see our own dignity as women and the shared dignity of all human persons. Only through the corrective lenses of the Incarnation and redemption can our vision of our nature be clarified, for it is these that teach us about unconditional and sacrificial love, as the Pope's letter clearly shows. Yet here lies a difficulty to which Mary Rousseau's paper had too little time to allude. Why was this elegant, compassionate document, so fecund with truth, received stillborn by so many, and especially by so many who possess (or should) the corrected vision offered by the Faith?

I believe that it is because of the same impoverished ability to love to which the document and Rousseau's paper point. Most of us simply cannot love in the way necessary for a true responsiveness to the teaching given us by the Holy Father in this letter.

Let us consider three of the positive examples that Dr. Rousseau sets forth to see how and perhaps why our society, including many women within the Church, still fails to love in the unconditional way to which the examples point.

Early in her paper, Rousseau draws our attention to section 5 of *Mulieris dignitatem*, subtitled "To Serve Means to Reign". The focus of this section is the Blessed Mother's *fiat*, her unconditional acceptance of God's loving will for her, expressive of an unconditional love for him. Mary's freedom, unsullied by the disorder of original sin, is a freedom exercised in the context of total self-confidence and trust in God. We, being sinful, are simply not free in that way, and yet God does invite us to just that freedom. It is for this that he has given us the Church and her sacraments which reconcile and reunite us to his will for us. Contrary to the cant of dissident women (and men), the Church is not the source of the imprisonment of our wills; she is the only sure source of their liberation, a source gained for us in part by the free self-giving of Mary's will exercised through her *fiat*. Why are we so reluctant to follow her example? Why do we persist in directing our vision toward the shadows of our own image of ourselves rather than toward the luminous image of God in his vision of us?

Some of the answer lies in Dr. Rousseau's example of the preoccupation with self-fulfillment which dominates the American feminist agenda.

Pope John Paul's concept of autoteleology, expressed through what the Pope calls "self-discovery", certainly validates an authentic role for self-fulfillment in human life. But, as Rousseau points out, when this is perverted by egocentricity, by a preference for one's own self-image over oneself as an image of God, it fails to be a proper *telos*, a proper end for man. I would, therefore, push the example of *Kramer vs. Kramer* even further. Its initial turn of plot points not only to a failure of self-giving love, but also to a complete absence of the sacrificial love modeled for us by our Lord and his Mother and proclaimed by Pope John Paul II in his letter on human suffering, *Salvifici doloris*.[2] This lack of sacrificial love is expressed not only in the perduring horror of abortion, that worst abandonment of one's child, but also in the insidious and growing horrors of euthanasia and suicide ("death with dignity") that characterize our "disposable" society. Add to these the self-gratifying demands to use unethical reproductive technologies to produce children "to order" and "for sale", and one sees a complete inability to suffer loss in oneself for the sake of the true good of another person. And yet, as *Salvifici doloris* clearly teaches, to choose freely to suffer for the sake of another is an act so contrary to irrational, deterministic nature that it is an act that must profoundly affirm and constitute human nature.[3] Only we can image God by loving in a sacrificial way. But again, we prefer our own self-image to the image of God within us, and our love is conditioned by that preference for ourselves. We are reluctant to love at our own expense.

Rousseau chooses the nuptial meaning of the human body as the central focus of her explanation of this letter on the dignity and vocation of woman. What a faith-filled and risky choice in a society like ours! Can it be that this document has not been embraced with the enthusiasm it deserves precisely because as a society we cannot grasp its roots in the Holy Father's understanding of human sexual activity as *holy*? Are we so jaded that we cannot see past the tawdry uses to which genital sexual activity has been put? That we cannot see that genital sex is only a part, albeit a compelling one, of what it means for humans to be sexed?

I must admit that I had to pause over this section of Rousseau's paper, asking how it applied to me, a woman never married. And then this occurred to me: in Houston we have active at this moment three serial rapists. The women who have been brutalized in my city seem to be without number. Our host city is similarly beleaguered. Crimes of violence against women are increasing at a frightening rate, while we continue to use women's bodies to sell radial tires and toothpaste. We have in most of our society lost the holiness of human sexuality, and women especially are paying a material and spiritual price that will never be recovered. When the Holy Father's letter teaches so compellingly of the true sacramental nature of sexual activity, of its proper integration into human life, why is it resisted and repudiated, especially by women? Here is an authentic sexuality, a sexuality worthy of rational free beings, who though less than angels are indeed so much more than beasts. Here is a sexuality to be given and shared by a communion of persons, by subjects who invite one another to share their inner lives, not just their outer bodies. Too much of sexual practice today stops at the outer shell of the body and thereby fails to image God and all his relationships in the beautiful ways set forth in Mary Rousseau's paper; for the body by itself is treated as just a thing, an object, and we are free to dominate and use mere things.[4]

As Mary Rousseau's paper drew me back into reflection on *Mulieris dignitatem*, its teachings, and the reception it has received, these were the not-completely-random thoughts and questions raised for me. Most valuable to me, though quite uncomfortable, was the realization that even we who perceive ourselves to be faithful to the Magisterium and docile to the teachings of our Holy Father have not really embraced this letter with the enthusiasm we should. I have looked at my own dignity as a woman of faith, and I have found something of a spiritual couch potato. I fear that I have often mistaken passivity for receptivity in my response to the initiative of our Lord and his Vicar, and I am grateful to be reminded of the truths to which I am called as a Catholic woman. As the communion of persons who are Catholic women faithful to these teachings, we must not become complacent about our fidelity. Neither initiative nor receptivity includes room for complacency. The woman of complacent faith may be a daughter of Eve, but she is no daughter of Mary of Nazareth! In her paper on the dignity and vocation of woman, Mary Rousseau has shown us once again our Father God, our Mother Mary, and our brother, the Christ. Let us always strive to grow in the family resemblance!

NOTES

[1] I refer particularly to Karol Wojtyla, *The Acting Person*, trans. Andrzej Potocki, vol. 10 of *Analecta Husserliana*, ed. Anna-Teresa Tymieniecka (Boston: D. Reidel, 1979); "The Person: Subject and Community", *Review of Metaphysics* 33 (Dec. 1979), pp. 273–308; and *Love and Responsibility*, trans. H. T. Willetts (New York: Farrar, Straus & Giroux, 1981).

[2] One must in fairness note that in the end of *Kramer vs. Kramer* the mother, although she does not return to home and family, does at least return her son to his father in recognition of the superior relationship that now exists between them. In this, at least there is a vestige of selfless love, if not the complete reality. Sadly, the film encourages us to be grateful for and even to admire the diminished reality.

[3] As I previously wrote in "The Value of Human Suffering: Pope John Paul II and Karol Wojtyla", *Proceedings of the American Catholic Philosophical Association* 50 (1986), pp. 185–93.

[4] Nowhere is this more evident than in the proabortionists' argument about a woman's "right" over her own body, as though the human body were a thing which one possesses like property rather than a constitutive element of the substantially united person. Leaving aside the weakness of the argument from the standpoint of property rights, its weakness from the standpoint of philosophical anthropology is one which any human being, and especially any woman, should fear. Namely, by reducing the body to a thing in some fashion distinct from and other than the person, this argument leaves the person vulnerable to all manner of abuses of the body from every quarter. This argument, in fact, plays into the hands of those who would reduce persons, especially women, to mere bodily objects, and one is somewhat surprised that the so-called feminists cannot see its implications beyond the narrow uses to which they put it.

JANET E. SMITH

FEMINISM, MOTHERHOOD, AND THE CHURCH

One might think that feminists would be pleased with John Paul II's *Mulieris dignitatem*, for many of his views seem compatible with their concerns. John Paul II, for instance, insists on the fundamental equality of men and women and maintains that references to God as male and as a father do not mean that God is masculine; God is neither masculine nor feminine. He offers a bold reading of Scripture, especially of the opening passages of Genesis wherein he sees the original relationship of man and woman, not as a hierarchical or patriarchal one, but one of equals. He teaches that the domination of women by men is the result of sin and that, in the redeemed world, men and women are equal.[1]

Yet, there is one element in particular of John Paul II's analysis of women that strikes feminists as truly retrograde. In *Mulieris dignitatem*, John Paul II states that "virginity and motherhood" are the "two particular dimensions of the fulfillment of the female personality" (sec. 17).[2] And in light of the fact that he speaks of virginity as a kind of "spiritual motherhood", it seems fair to say that John Paul II considers motherhood to be the peculiar vocation of women. This (and the refusal to admit women to the priesthood) is the crucial sticking point for feminists. Some feminists, for instance, argue that the institution of motherhood is characterized by an oversentimental idealization. Consider the comments of a feminist who finds the Magisterium's "idealized image" of women's "nurturing, maternal qualities" to be "strangely implausible" and "separated as by a chasm from the ordinary experience of an increasing number of women and men".[3] Consider, as well, Gregory Baum's comments on *Mulieris dignitatem*:

> ... missing in the Letter is a longer reflection on the sign of the times, i.e., the presence of women in *public life*. Today women no longer define themselves through their potential for motherhood. Women continue to be good mothers, but they include in their self-definition, the full human vocation, including their role as thinkers, actors, and leaders.[4]

Baum's remark appears in a kind of postscript to a feminist collection of essays on motherhood, *Motherhood: Experience, Institution, Theology*, a volume of the theological journal *Concilium*. A perusal of the essays in this book suggests that Baum understates the feminist view of motherhood. The evidence of this volume suggests that feminists do not simply reject motherhood as a defining characteristic of women; rather it suggests that at least some feminists come perilously close to repudiating motherhood completely as an appropriate vocation for women. Consider a statement in the introduction to *Motherhood: Experience, Institution, Theology* which asserts: "It is the institution of motherhood that keeps ... women and children, under patriarchal control, and disempowers women."[5] In a patriarchal world, motherhood is seen as a biological function that relegates women entirely to the private sphere; women are not welcome in the public square. Children thus come to look upon mothers—and by extension women—as second-class. One commentator tells us that: "As the earliest representative of the world, women are seen as part of nature, as nonhuman and unpersons. . . ."[6] Women, seen to have value only as mothers, are thus undervalued by society. Nearly all of the authors represented in this book find the value of motherhood to be very suspect, for they believe motherhood to be the invention of a patriarchal and androcentric worldview, an invention that, by foisting all childcare on women, serves to keep them housebound and outside the spheres of power.

Now let me register a caveat here. There are almost as many brands of feminism as there are feminists. Thus, many feminists will deny that the values and attitudes I ascribe to feminists are true of them. And they may be right, individually. But it is from reading the publications of the leaders of the feminist movement, of their scholars and thinkers, that I have drawn my conclusions; it is their views that pervade the women's magazines and the media and eventually dictate the terms of the public debate and form the values of the young. Thus, it is their views that deserve analysis and confrontation. Much of my analysis is based upon the essays appearing in the text mentioned above, *Motherhood: Experience, Institution, Theology*. It sets out quite explicitly how these leading feminists evaluate motherhood. The contributions to this text (with a few notable exceptions) are universally critical of motherhood.

Much of this essay will be a description of the current feminist evaluation of motherhood, an evaluation that, as noted earlier, is largely negative. But what I hope to show is that there is a paradox at the center of the feminist agenda. The paradox is this: many of the concerns of feminism, seen in a certain light, are precisely the concerns traditionally considered characteristic of mothers. In spite of the anger and bitterness and hatred directed against motherhood in much feminist literature, there is a poignant undercurrent in some of the themes that repeatedly emerge. Many of the yearnings expressed, many of the concerns so fervently held, are those one would expect to find among mothers. For instance, feminists are very disturbed by the failure of all to get the recognition they deserve; they are appalled by poverty, especially the poverty of mothers with children; they are horrified by child abuse and sexual abuse. Are not these very close to the concerns of a true mother's heart?

Thus, I shall argue that the feminist repudiation of the values of motherhood is a terrible mistake; that a feminism true to the nature of women would radically change some portions of the feminist agenda. For instance, it would not have as one of its central thrusts the full employment of women in the public sector. Rather, a feminism true to the nature of women would recognize that the worst injustice done to women is the severe undervaluation of the values of motherhood. It would not join in an increasing rejection of motherhood in modern American culture;[7] rather, it would work to protect and foster the role and place of mothers in our society. Nor would the promotion of the values of motherhood necessitate abandoning all the items currently on the feminist agenda; much of this essay will be sorting through the feminist agenda to identify which items on it conflict with the values of motherhood and which are more likely to be achieved through promotion of the values of motherhood.

In the final portion of this essay, I will argue that it is inappropriate for feminists to reject the Church's teaching on sexuality, a teaching designed precisely to protect the values of motherhood. I will argue that insofar as feminism rejects the Church's teaching on sexuality, it facilitates rather than battles the evils against women so prominent in Western culture.

I

My reading of feminist literature suggests that there are four fundamental characteristics of feminism:[8] the first we might call the "truth criterion" plank of the platform; the second is the political plank; the third, the ethical; the fourth, the symbolic. Let me explain these four planks and demonstrate how motherhood, in the view of many feminists, coheres with none of them.

First, feminism has its own standard of truth. As mentioned above, fundamental to feminism is its claim that women have been oppressed and exploited; thus, everything is judged according to its truthfulness in reflecting the oppression and exploitation of women. I once attended a feminist conference where it was clear that the speakers eschewed the words "true" and "false"; they registered their approval or disapproval of

FEMINISM, MOTHERHOOD, AND THE CHURCH   45

claims by deeming them "acceptable" or "unacceptable": that is, acceptable or unacceptable to the feminist agenda. Since the feminist agenda is focused on the liberation of women, all claims to truth, both philosophical and theological, are judged against this standard question: Does the claim being made advance the liberation of women? The final test for the truth of texts or claims is women's experience. Consider this comment by Lisa Cahill:

> Evidence about women from the Bible and tradition is inextricably colored by patriarchal culture and must be complemented by, and even meet the final test of, women's own experiences of oppression, liberation, and transformative justice. The appeal to experience as the paramount authority for feminist thought raises serious epistemological issues, shared by feminist thinkers with other postmodern theorists, regarding the objectivity or "truth" value of knowledge and moral judgment.[9]

That is, feminists use only their own experience as the criterion of truth and thereby reject any claims that there is an objective truth apart from their experience.

The stories of Scripture, for instance, are often rejected or reinterpreted since they are believed to be a product of male writers enculturated with the values of patriarchy. Feminists allow only those interpretations of Scripture that fit with the claim that women have been universally oppressed and exploited and are in need of liberation. This has led to some extraordinary, not to say blasphemous, interpretations of Scripture. For instance, some feminist theologians suggest that the conception of Christ was not the work of the Holy Spirit.[10] They seriously argue that Mary conceived Christ through a rape. This would put Mary squarely in the ranks of the downcast, oppressed, and marginalized. These scholars argue that God chose to send his Son in this fashion to show his complete solidarity with the downcast, oppressed, and marginalized. These feminists arrive at this interpretation not on the basis of new discoveries that have led them to a new truth, though they use scholarly apparatus to support their claims. Rather, they sought a new interpretation to fit what they believe to be the experience of women and find this interpretation "acceptable" because, in their view, it advances the feminist agenda.

The reality of motherhood does not easily cohere with the feminist criterion of truth, based on the assertion that all women have been exploited and oppressed. One problem is that many, if not most, mothers do not experience their lives as ones of exploitation and repression; they enjoy their children and the challenges that being a mother brings. Surely, they fight bouts of exhaustion and discouragement and occasionally of boredom, but, nonetheless, they rejoice in the love-drenched and meaningful life that is made possible to them through their children. Many feminists tend to consider such women unreflective and kind of Uncle Toms or Aunt Mabels, if you will. They claim that their experience of family and men is authoritative, an experience of family and of men that seems to have been quite negative. They tend to discount the experience of women who find fulfillment in marriage and family and who have had satisfying relationships with the men central to their lives: their fathers, with their boyfriends, husbands, and male coworkers. This experience does not count in the articulation of the feminist agenda.

The second plank of the feminist platform is a political one; feminists intend to bring about vast political and social change and to reform society so that women have full access to all spheres of public life. Affirmative action, for instance, is a key instrument for this purpose. And, of course, so is daycare. Feminists generally are more concerned to see the workplace restructured so that it allows women with small children to remain at the job than to restructure the economic system so that it allows mothers with small children to stay at home.

The feminist program also entails reforming the "thought systems" that legitimate what they see to be the present unjust social order. One thought system that needs to be reformed is the notion that motherhood is a worthy calling for women.

FEMINISM, MOTHERHOOD, AND THE CHURCH   47

Many feminists are hostile to stay-at-home mothers. They seem to consider stay-at-home mothers as the witless dupes of patriarchy. Many feminists seem to think that all true power is in the public sphere, and they seem to have abandoned the age-old wisdom that the hand that rocks the cradle, rules the world. Feminists find such "wisdom" offensive and a tool of patriarchy to keep women away from the true sources of power.

In my view, feminists have lost sight of the distinctively feminine insight that leadership and public office are not the only or even the chief paths to true power—the power to shape hearts and minds. Many young women in the '50s and '60s did not envy young men their fixation on career and the workplace; having a career meant being on someone else's schedule, of marching to the beat of someone else's drum. Many young women tended to have the view that women had the better part: women were able to have children, to stay at home and care for them, to be their own bosses and to volunteer for whatever causes they felt worthy. Admittedly, it was widely agreed that mothers were greatly underappreciated and to some degree this was a source of resentment. Betty Friedan's groundbreaking book, *The Feminist Mystique*, argued that motherhood had been trivialized after World War II and that women were given to having as their highest ideal floors free from waxy buildup. Her prescription for relief from the doldrums of motherhood was that women pursue stimulating careers. But many women have found: (1) stimulating careers are often incompatible with motherhood and (2) many career options, such as bank teller or grocery clerk, are just not very stimulating. In spite of its hardships, many women found, and continue to find, that whatever stimulation, prestige, and financial reward careers offer, motherhood can be a role with its own intrinsic and unsurpassable rewards. They do not seek a more rewarding career but seek to have the value of motherhood rightly appreciated.

Many young women of the '50s and '60s who had seen their mothers lead rich and rewarding lives as full-time mothers, did not immediately join ranks with the feminist movement. They thought the movement would take a different turn; that it would not seek to thrust all women into the workplace, but that it would seek rightful recognition for the contribution of mothers and ways to encourage men to take a greater role in childrearing and the work of the home. They were surprised to learn that the feminist movement seemed to accept the view that motherhood was of little value, that the only work worth doing was that for which one was paid. At one time in Canada, there was a movement called "Wages for Housewives", a movement that seemed to grant that unless one was paid for work, one's work was worthless. But mothers tend to think there is no price that can be put on their work: it is work done out of love and should be repaid only by love. In fact, I have often thought that many women tend to regard any work that one gets paid for as worth less than the work one does for free—work that one does out of love. Motherhood, of course, is filled with such work.

Feminists have their own ethical agenda, necessitated in part by their political agenda. Essential to the feminist agenda are abortion, divorce, sterilization, contraception, and the new reproductive technologies; these, they believe, liberate a woman from the evils of an androcentric world. They give women a full range of reproductive choices. And, not incidentally, women who have recourse to contraception and abortion, tend to have fewer children. In the view of many feminists, that is all to the good; for how can women assume positions of power and influence if they are having and taking care of children? Yet, on the other hand, although feminists reject motherhood as defining of women, they hail the new reproductive technologies since they expand women's choices in regard to motherhood—now single women, the infertile, and lesbians can mother children if they so choose. Motherhood is not valued for itself, but simply as another option or choice that women would like to have; they want whatever children they have to be carefully planned and chosen. Women who have children as they come, so to speak, perhaps with a bit of spacing through ecological breastfeeding, appear to be complete and inexplicable anachronisms to the modern feminist who carefully orchestrates all elements of her life. Contraception, abortion, and some of the new reproductive technologies, such as the possibility of artificial wombs, are, along with daycare, answers to the feminist dream: the possibility of planned reproduction with minimum inconvenience to women, with minimum interruption to one's career.

Feminism not only has had a distinctive, practical ethical agenda, it also seeks to reform ethical theory. Many feminists want to argue that women have a distinctive ethical perspective. They argue that, whereas men have a special concern for objective and impersonal justice, women have a special concern for compassion, caring, and nurturing (I think there is certainly some truth in this analysis). They argue that these values ought to be as central to ethical analysis as the concern for impersonal justice. This claim, though, seems to work at cross-purposes with other elements of the feminist agenda. For they also reject the value of being self-sacrificing and see this as another value foisted on women so that they will put themselves more fully in service of men. Yet, compassion, caring, and nurturing have always been closely allied with self-sacrifice and self-denial and, indeed, with motherhood. Thus, feminists have floundered in their attempts to establish a distinctive feminist ethic; they find it difficult to extol the quality of "nurturing" for instance, while denying the value of self-denial and the value of motherhood.

Finally, the fourth plank of feminism seeks to redo the symbolism of the Church since feminists consider the Church to be a great threat to their goals. At one time, of course, feminists were clamoring for the right to speak of God as Mother as well as Father. But that demand is beginning to evaporate. Motherhood, with its association with patriarchy, does not project the correct symbolism for women. Feminists do not find the portrait of God as Mother to be any more attractive than the portrait of God as Father.[11] Furthermore, many feminists claim that women do not have a positive experience of being mothered and, therefore, to project motherhood as an ideal for women or as a symbol of God would not be positing a favorable image at all. Feminists are groping for suitable symbols; they speak of the need to use positively other female relationships as symbols, such as sisterhood, midwifery, etc.

Feminist theologians, of course, find one of the chief sources of oppression of women in the Church's exclusion of women from the priesthood. They think this teaching reflects a view that women are unsuited to do the most important work of the Church. The Church has always protested that the work of mothering is a work of tremendous importance for the Church and contends that the exclusion of women from the priesthood in no way suggests the intellectual or spiritual inferiority of women. But such protests sound to feminists like only another attempt to keep women in their place.

The feminist agenda as portrayed here has been rejected by many women. Yet, even those who reject the main lines of the feminist agenda allow that in some respects feminists have done women a service. They have alerted many to the fact that women have many talents in addition to those needed by a wife and mother. They have opened many public and private spheres to the influence of women, and they have exposed how some societal and cultural institutions and practices (such as pornography) have exploited women and children. They have succeeded, to some extent, in getting men to take greater responsibility for home and family as well as career. Nonetheless, it becomes increasingly obvious that some of the advances of feminism have been bought at the cost of denigrating some of the noblest and most distinctive qualities of women; that there has been a tendency in feminism itself to undervalue the distinctively feminine, certainly insofar as the distinctively feminine is closely allied with motherhood.

II

Motherhood, then, takes a great battering at the hands of feminists. The feminist dismissal of the distinctively feminine was clear early on in such works as *The Second Sex* by Simone de Beauvoir. This dismissal nearly always goes hand in hand with a rejection of what is natural. De Beauvoir evinced the typical feminist disdain for "what is natural" (a disdain that is true to her existentialist philosophy): "One does not arrive in the world as a woman, but one becomes a woman. No biological, mental, or economic fate determines the form that a female human being takes on in the womb of society."[12] She speaks with great envy of the lives of males—lives that are defined by work—which is "transcendent" and takes men out of the world —rather than by family—which is "immanent" and confines one to this world:

> Because he [the husband] is productively employed, he passes beyond the interests of the family toward those of society and gives the family a future by contributing to building a future for the social whole. He is an embodiment of transcendence. The wife is left with responsibility for preserving the species and managing the household, which means nothing but immanence.[13]

Indeed, some feminists deny that motherhood is a natural role for women at all. One feminist sociologist argues that "mothering is not inborn or natural, but induced by social structures and reproduced by psychological processes".[14] Here, we get a glimpse at the feminist hatred for nature; feminists speak of "anachronistic laws of nature" which force them to conceive children as the result of sexual intercourse. Indeed, since motherhood is a quintessentially natural state, in some respects, feminism has come to hate nature. One radical American feminist calls for the elimination of genital sexual characteristics since, even in the animal kingdom, females are generally subordinated to males because of these differences. She understands "reproduction" to enslave women and observes: "Pregnancy is the temporary deformation of the body of the individual for the sake of the species."[15] As mentioned above, for this reason, many feminists have been extremely enthusiastic about the new birth technologies and look to the day when all baby-making can take place apart from a woman's body. As one Catholic feminist remarked: "Until the time when human beings are produced in laboratories, instead of having to be brought into the world by women, men will have an essential advantage over women, and they will exploit it. Until that time, the notion of 'equal rights' will remain an unrealizable dream."[16] The most radical element of feminism, then (which unfortunately all too soon becomes mainstream feminism), is taking a turn toward such total rejection of what is distinctively female, toward such a total rejection of motherhood, that it seeks the complete obliteration of natural childbearing.

Yet, the essays in the *Concilium* volume mentioned above do not universally reject motherhood. There is a radically discordant note in some of the essays, a note that is in manifest conflict with the attitudes toward motherhood delineated above. An essay by a woman from the Third World is a paean to motherhood. In describing herself, she states:

> I am a Ghanaian and an Akan with both my parents and their parents on both sides belonging to mother-centred groups. My political and economic status in Akan structures depend on who my mother is. I am who I am because of who my mother is. I have no biological children but I am the first of my parents' nine children. Any Akan daughter will tell you what that means. I have not experienced motherhood but I know what "mothering" means. I have accompanied my mother through her motherhood. Motherhood has not made my mother poor. *My mother is rich.* She has a community of people whose joys and sorrows are hers. I am rich because I have this community and hold a special place in it. I am not a mother but I have children.
>
> To many ears this sounds folklorique, a glorification of a culture, sublimation of instincts and many such explanations. For me this is life. . . . Mothering is a religious duty. It is what a good socio-political and economic system should be about if the human beings entrusted to the state are to be fully human, nurtured to care for, and take care of themselves, one another, and of their environments. Biological motherhood embodies all of this for the Akan as for many African peoples.[17]

Mercy Amba Oduyoye, the author of this essay, agrees that Western values are responsible for the exploitation of women, but puts an interesting twist on the charge; she states:

> The anti-baby economy of the North is preached in the South, through these economic measures and quite overtly, since at least in one African country young women can only get employment in the formal sector if they can show that they are on an antimotherhood drug. So the message is clear, if you do not want to be poor or become impoverished do not become a mother. In God's economy, the human being is a necessary and integral part. God gave the management of the earth to the Earth— beings that God created.[18]

Note that she speaks of contraception as an "antimotherhood drug"—what an apt description! (Let us no longer speak of contraceptive pills but of antimotherhood pills.) She speaks about how the imported Western culture puts no value on the work of the home and how Western medical procedures abuse women. She asks:

> Why would women submit to radiation, Depo-Provera, sex selection and other hazards of contemporary reproductive technology and genetic engineering that invade and violate their bodies and therefore impoverish their sense of personhood by treating them as objects of research and experiments? In most countries it is women who are exploited in this genetic technology.[19]

Mercy Amba Oduyoye exhibits the love of children so characteristic of the Third World. This love is so manifest that it does not escape the notice of the most militant feminists. It was watching women and families in Third World countries that led Germaine Greer to observe that most of the world's delight and most of the world's reasons for existing comes from children, especially in nonmaterialistic nations.[20] This is a truth most feminists are loath to entertain, let alone endorse.

Another writer in the *Concilium* volume expresses grave reservations about the new birth technologies, for reasons that smack of an appreciation of some of the values of motherhood.

While she acknowledges that the new birth technologies can be deemed a good insofar as they multiply the choices that one has, she worries that the replacement of the natural processes has a negative aspect as well. She speaks about the dangers of wanting to produce perfect children; about the likely further marginalization of the imperfect. She notes that: "[In these processes] nature's and women's reproductive capacity is completely absent and is replaced by high-technological processes. The human being is here a technical quality product as opposed to a piece of art".[21] She observes that:

> The perfect human being who develops his character with genetically manipulated characteristics, and the foetus that no longer needs a mother for its development, reveal a certain view of mankind: that of the self-sufficient, abstract individual who lives and acts independently from his environment.[22]

She deems this view of mankind as one characteristic of a patriarchal culture and suggests that women have another view that emphasizes attachment and intimacy, and she sees pregnancy as the condition that really highlights this view. While it may be that males are not as individualistic as she allows, she is certainly correct that it is women, and especially mothers, who value bonding, attachment, and intimacy.

That we find these essays laudatory of motherhood side by side with a wholesale rejection of motherhood should not be completely surprising. Perhaps nature cannot be denied. That is, perhaps the maternal nature of women is so strong it will emerge, no matter how ardent the efforts to repress it. Even in the texts that are most hostile to motherhood, we can find themes that resonate with a yearning for the values of motherhood. The ethical agenda, for instance, almost in spite of itself, values compassion, caring, and nurturing; the political agenda, when not focused on affirmative action, also aspires to the elimination of pornography and other forms of child and sexual abuse. It labors to find means to free women and children from the debilitating effects of poverty. The symbolic agenda, in spite of its ambivalence about motherhood, keeps striving to find room for exalting the distinctively feminine. The values of motherhood, then, are implicitly present in many portions of the feminist agenda.

It is perhaps the lived experience of motherhood that most threatens to undercut the feminist rejection of motherhood by feminists (that threatens to annihilate the "truth criterion" of feminism). Recent years have seen a not-so-surprising defection in the feminist ranks from the pure feminist agenda. More and more we read about women who, after achieving many of the goals most important to feminism, somewhat repudiate these goals. They have come to see that motherhood satisfies some of their deeper yearnings and acknowledge that some of the ideals of feminism have left them empty. The fact is that many and perhaps most women, even feminists, enjoy being mothers. A telling editorial appeared in the *Chicago Tribune* shortly after Barbara Bush gave her commencement address at Wellesley. Written by a 1975 Wellesley graduate, it spoke of the testimony given by several women at their fifteen-year reunion. These women told how, although they had had major successes in their careers, they eventually abandoned career for the sake of their families. The editorial writer accused Wellesley of preparing them for careers but not preparing them to meet the needs of their souls.[23]

III

While some feminists may be coming to reject the view of the most radical feminists that motherhood is degrading to and exploitative of women, few, if any, see Mother Church as anything but oppressive of women. An honest look at the Church might disclose another picture. Certainly, most feminists are rooted in the concrete and have little interest in the theoretical. Their evaluation of the Church may be based primarily on how she has historically and actually treated women. Not being a historian, I am not prepared to comment on such a historically based critique of the Church. I suspect, though, that, in some ways, the Church has been in the vanguard in recognizing women's talents—the accomplishments over the centuries of nuns, as missionaries, as teachers, hospital administrators, social workers, college presidents, and so forth—demand great respect. My focus is upon the *teaching* of the Church, and I make the claim that the *teaching* of the Church has been and is one that has great respect for women and has waged battles with nearly every age and combatted theories and practices that denigrate women.

The Church's teaching on motherhood has undergone a kind of development. It has not changed in the sense of having been reversed: rather, we currently see more clearly some dimensions of that teaching that have gone unarticulated before. The truth that we now see, or are coming to see, is one that has been there to see all along, though we have not always seen it. What I want to claim here is something similar to a statement made by Mercy Amba Oduyoye, the African author cited earlier. Her thesis is—more or less—that a culture or society is to be judged as a success only insofar as it is structured in such a way as to provide the conditions for mothers to do their work well. The evils that have been generated as a consequence of the breakdown of family life have brought this truth into higher relief. The evils generated by the elevation of the goods of freedom, by the deification of the autonomy of the individual, are clearly evils that strike at the goods of the family. A radical, atomistic liberty may warrant pornography, abortion, divorce, licentious entertainment, homosexuality, etc.; a concern for the goods of the family does not. It is no surprise that we have a group called Mothers Against Drunk Driving and that it is mothers who are leading the fight against obscene lyrics in rock music. Furthermore, motherhood properly engaged in requires fatherhood and results in families; that is, in communities that work for the good of others as well as for oneself. Sociological studies convincingly demonstrate that those who are blessed to have been raised in intact households with loving parents and brothers and sisters are much less inclined to succumb to the evils of teenage pregnancy, alcoholism, drug addiction, and the vast variety of psychological maladies to which our age is so prone. Paradoxically, we often begin to see truths more clearly, not when we are living them more authentically —for then we rather take them for granted—but when they are threatened.

Motherhood, seen in its true Christian light, is one of the most valued if not the most valued role among all roles possible for humans in the purely human realm. It is the source of great human goods, beginning with the great good of life and extending to the good of unconditional love for the individual. God fashioned the whole universe for the sake of sharing it with humans. He wishes to share his goodness with humans. The bringing forth of new life, then, is an activity very near the divine act of creation. Nor, of course, is it sufficient simply to bring forth new life; this new life must also be educated and formed in such a way as to merit eternal salvation. The love of a true mother wants what is best for her child, and what is best for her child is union with God. Thus, true mothers and God are totally in cahoots. Their job is one and the same: bringing new souls to salvation. Fathers, of course, have an equal responsibility for achieving this end, but mothers seem to have it in a more direct and immediate way. After all, when God speaks of his undying love for mankind, he compares himself to a mother; Isaiah 49:15 states: "Can a mother forget her infant, be without tenderness for the child of her womb? Even should she forget, I will never forget you."[24]

Because of original sin, we dwell in a fallen world, and not all is as it should be. That being the case, in a world where values are upside down, it is no surprise that motherhood has been denigrated. Thus, the Judeo-Christian message, which seeks to restore the natural order, has been one that labors to exalt the role of motherhood. The creation of women made possible the institution of marriage—an institution that is not solely for childbearing; certainly it is an institution that meets the deeper needs of the human person for intimacy and love. Still, one of the deeper needs humans have is to become an adult, and one of the paths to becoming an adult is to become a parent; it is also a path to further intimacy and love, both with one's spouse and with one's children. One of the great things that spouses can do for each other is to make each other parents. The very word "matrimony" suggests something of the centrality of parenthood to marriage; its roots are the Latin words, *mater*, or mother, and *munus*, a word meaning mission, role, or assignment. Matrimony, then, means "the mission of the mother". This suggests that matrimony is the institution designed to allow a mother (and by extension, the father, too) to perform the mission that God has given to her. Any attack on motherhood is an attack on God's own work.

Much of the preserving of the good of sexuality and childbearing has been done through the Church's teaching on sexual ethics. In a certain sense, the commitment to protecting the values of motherhood has informed the whole of the Church's teaching on sexuality. The Church disapproves of any sexual activity that is divorced from the possibility of procreation; she disapproves of any sexual activity that is not a part of family life.

Thus, in a certain sense, a woman's sexuality defines Christian moral teaching on sexuality. George Gilder in his remarkable book, *Men and Marriage* (a second, much-revised edition of his *Sexual Suicide*), argues that civilization depends upon the subjugation of men to women's sexual identity.[25] In brief, he argues that men tend by nature (fallen nature, I might add) to be promiscuous and to be satisfied with quick sexual encounters with women whom they view only as sex objects. It is when men begin to think about having progeny that they begin to look upon women as persons—specifically, as the person who will be mother to their children. They then work on making themselves individuals worthy to win the love of a woman who will be a worthy mother to their children. The capacity of women for motherhood, then, is what shapes men into responsible adults. Perhaps John Paul II has something of this in mind when in *Mulieris dignitatem* he states that the man "has to learn his own 'fatherhood' from the mother" (no. 18). At any rate, in the Christian schema, "patriarchy" does not mean that men govern to satisfy their own selfish desires. In a Christian "patriarchy" or "rule of the father", properly understood, then, the fathers are not to dominate over mothers and children. Mothers and children have a kind of primacy since all "ruling" or work is to be done primarily on their behalf. Fathers work to shape the world so that mothers may do their work well.

What feminists seem to fail to see is that if people were living in accord with the Christian understanding of God, with the Christian understanding of human nature, and with the Christian moral norms of sexuality, there would not be exploitation of women, sexual abuse of women and children, women with children left abandoned to an impoverished existence. Rather, the Christian view requires that men be true to women and respect their sexuality. And think of the evils that would be greatly reduced in this world if spouses were living in accord with the Church's teaching on marriage—so closely linked to its teaching on motherhood. Again, many of the modern world's ills can be traced to broken homes, to dysfunctional families, to a failure of mothers and fathers to be true to their vocations. Healthy and whole families, on the other hand, contribute greatly to the nurturing of virtue and self-esteem and thus to the solving of many of society's ills.

Antimotherhood proposals, then, contribute to rather than solve the world's problems. They don't do much for women either. Among these proposals, as mentioned, are demands for full freedom of divorce, full access to contraception, sterilization, and abortion. Since feminists seek to achieve a maximum of choices for women—which they equate with liberation or freedom—the choice of all these is necessary. But what they are sacrificing for fairly unsavory "liberation" is a respect for a woman's dignity and worth. For instance, divorce and abortion are rarely, if ever, the result of loving and respectful relationships and nearly always, if not always, the result of very exploitative and damaging relationships. Women and children suffer the most from divorce; the divorced male's income generally expands; the women and her children are left in poverty. It is the woman who undergoes an abortion, often because she cannot depend upon the father of the child to support her and their child. Contraception—antimotherhood drugs and devices—in most of its forms, treats the female anatomy as if it were a terrible mistake. The Church disallows divorce and promotes faithful marriages; the Church disallows abortion and maintains that all life must be welcomed; the Church forbids contraception and sterilization for she finds both sexual intercourse and its natural outcome to be among God's great gifts. Fidelity, welcomed babies, and natural means of family planning are greatly conducive to human happiness in no small part because they are in accord with respect for a woman's dignity. Natural family planning, for instance, requires planning a couple's sexual life, not around male sexual urges, but around a woman's fertility cycle. Most couples who use NFP report a significant improvement in their overall relationship as the result of this submission of their sexual lives to the nature of their fertility.

Catholic teaching on sexuality and marriage, then, is very much centered on respect for women, their needs, and their missions in life. Again, it can even be said that all of the work of this world is good only to the extent that it advances the work of mothers—work that should be directed ultimately to the well-being of the world's children. But it is not because motherhood requires a kind of submission on the part of men that women should embrace the role of motherhood. Rather, women should embrace motherhood because it is the role that God has designed for women.

Nor is it a role conducive simply to helping God populate his Kingdom with the souls of women and men's offspring. Rather, motherhood is a role most conducive to aiding women in advancing their own salvation. Motherhood has special qualities allied with it, qualities which are very close to the very qualities that Christianity seeks to foster. While it is sadly true that many today have had mothers who do not exemplify the virtues of motherhood, it is nonetheless true that others are blessed enough to have had mothers who remarkably approach anyone's ideal of motherhood. Certainly, it is true that we are living in an age where children are sadly neglected and often greatly wounded at the hands of their parents, parents who are barely adults themselves either in respect of age or of maturity. Some of them have suffered from very bad parenting. But this reality has not completely obscured our sense and our memory that it is possible for parents, and, it must be admitted, particularly mothers, to be spectacular examples of self-giving. One senses that without the perversions and distortions of our modern world, there would be many more such mothers, since it is so very natural for mothers to give their all for their children. To say that it is natural, is not to suggest that it comes easily; all of us are fundamentally selfish, and it takes a great deal of self-denial and self-control to acquire the virtues needed to become a good parent, but having children gives one special incentive, the incentive of love and responsibility, to exercise self-denial and to practice self-control.

Mothers are capable of being unconditional lovers who love their children simply because they exist. Of course, they will rejoice in the successes of their children and sorrow in their hardships, but they will love them ardently in season and out. They labor hard to make life smooth for their children which, of course, means that at times they must allow life to be hard for their children. Mothers become selfless and self-sacrificing as they get up late at night to feed their babies, to care for a sick child, to comfort a distressed adolescent or a grieving adult child. Again, God compares himself to a mother when he speaks of his desire to comfort mankind: in Isaiah 66:12–13, we read, "As nurslings, you shall be carried in her arms, and fondled in her lap; as a mother comforts her son, so will I comfort you; in Jerusalem you shall find your comfort." Mothers, out of love for their children, attempt to nourish all the uniquely wonderful qualities of their children and try to help their children acquire all the virtues. Christian mothers, of course, are most concerned to raise their children to be good Christians and thereby raise good citizens, husbands, wives, friends, and coworkers as well. And what work could be more important—or fulfilling—than that?

As was mentioned above, feminists claim that it is a patriarchal society that urges women to develop the virtues of self-denial and self-sacrifice. To feminists, these are not attractive qualities, but I suspect this is because they associate these qualities too closely with a kind of passivity, a lack of initiative, and perhaps even a lack of imagination. Yet, certainly these negative qualities are not in the least inherent in mothering and, in fact, are inimicable to true mothering. In *Mulieris dignitatem*, John Paul II reminds us that "to serve, is to reign"; he notes that a life of "self-giving" is of the very essence of the Christian life. And, as sketched above, motherhood is the natural institution most designed to foster the quintessential Christian virtue of self-giving. Although our times make it especially difficult for women to foster the virtues that motherhood in particular makes possible, it should be clear that women and men would do well to seek the virtues of motherhood.

The Church's focus on the value of motherhood and its essential role in defining the vocation of women does not, of course, mean that it is the *only* vocation appropriate for women. Again, witness the public role played by many nuns. But what the Church insists upon is that public work not be deemed more important than the work of the home, nor that the work of the home be sacrificed for public work. As *Familiaris consortio* states:

> There is no doubt that the equal dignity and responsibility of men and women fully justifies women's access to public functions. On the other hand the true advancement of women requires that clear recognition be given to the value of their maternal

and family role, by comparison with all other public roles and all other professions. Furthermore, these roles and professions should be harmoniously combined, if we wish the evolution of society and culture to be truly and fully human.[26]

Moreover, women are to retain their femininity in whatever pursuits they engage:

> ... all of this does not mean for women a renunciation of their femininity or an imitation of the male role, but the fullness of true feminine humanity which should be expressed in their activity, whether in the family or outside of it, without disregarding the differences of customs and cultures in this sphere.[27]

These passages seem to echo some of the views of Edith Stein who held, "There is no profession which cannot be practised by a woman."[28] She also insisted that the gifts of femininity should be brought to the workplace:

> Basically the same spiritual attitude which the wife and mother need is needed here also, except that it is extended to a wider working circle and mostly to a changing area of people; for that reason, the perspective is detached from the vital bond of blood relationship and more highly elevated on the spiritual level.[29]

Women are called to motherhood, whether it be physical or spiritual.

Feminists have a great deal of righteous and rightful indignation against many evils; they have, however, embarked on an agenda more designed to aid and abet the perpetrators of these evils than to combat them. The Church shares the feminist outrage at the exploitation and degradation of women that has characterized much of both Western and Eastern civilization. She, too, decries sexual abuse, poverty, and abuse of the environment. The Church, too, wishes women to achieve complete fulfillment of their talents and gifts. But the Church thinks that only a full appreciation for motherhood can secure the true liberation of women. It is regrettable, indeed, that feminists have joined the forces of those ready to scrap the values of motherhood rather than joining the Church in her relentless effort to protect the values of motherhood, values that protect the true dignity of women.

NOTES

[1] See Gregory Baum, "Bulletin: The Apostolic Letter *Mulieris dignitatem*" in *Motherhood: Experience, Institution, Theology*, ed. Anne Carr and Elisabeth Schussler Fiorenza (Edinburgh: T & T Clark, 1989), wherein he expresses some appreciation for these views in *Mulieris dignitatem*.

[2] For a translation of the encyclical *Mulieris dignitatem*, see "On the Dignity and Vocation of Women" *Origins* 18:17 (October 6, 1988), pp. 263–83 or the edition published by Daughters of St. Paul (Boston: Daughters of St. Paul, 1988).

[3] Margaret O'Brien Steinfels, "The Church and its Public Life", *America* 160 (1989), pp. 553–54.

[4] Baum, "Bulletin", in *Motherhood*, p. 149.

[5] *Motherhood*, p. 3.

[6] *Motherhood*, p. 18.

[7] For an excellent analysis of this rejection see Maggie Gallagher, *The Enemies of Eros* (Chicago: Bonus Books, 1989).

[8] For a good review of feminist literature, at least of the theological literature, see Lisa Cahill, "Notes on Moral Theology: 1989; Feminist Ethics", *Theological Studies* 51 (1990), pp. 49–64.

[9] Cahill, p. 51.

[10] See, for instance, Jane Shabery, "The Foremothers and the Mother of Jesus", in *Motherhood*, pp. 112–20.

[11] See Johanna Kohn-Roelin, "Mother–Daughter–God", *Motherhood*, pp. 64–72.

[12] Quoted from Manfred Hauke, *Women in the Priesthood?* (San Francisco: Ignatius Press, 1988), 34; citing Simone de Beauvoir, *Das andere Geschlecht, Sitte und Sexus der Frau* (Hamburg, 1952), p. 285.

[13] Ibid., p. 35, citing *Das andere Geschlecht*, p. 432.

[14] *Motherhood*, p. 17.

[15] Ibid., p. 38, citing Shulamith Firestone, *Frauenbefreiung und sexuelle Revolution* (Frankfurt, 1975), p. 19.

[16] Ibid., p. 42, citing Anita Reoper, *Ist gott ein Mann? Ein Gespraech mit Karl Rahner* (Düsseldorf, 1979), p. 51.

[17] Mercy Amba Oduyoye, "Poverty and Motherhood" in *Motherhood*, p. 23.

[18] Ibid., p. 29.

[19] Ibid., p. 26.

[20] Germaine Greer, *Sex and Destiny: The Politics of Human Fertility* (New York: Harper and Row, 1984).

[21] Dorry De Beijer, "Motherhood and Reproductive Technology", in *Motherhood*, p. 78.

²² Ibid.

²³ Jessica Gress-Wright, "Feminism: Beyond the Second Stage", *First Things* 6 (October 1990): pp. 12–14.

²⁴ In this article, translations for passages from Scripture are taken from the *New American Bible* (Camden, N.J.: Thomas Nelson, Inc., 1971).

²⁵ George Gilder, *Men and Marriage* (Gretna: Pelican Publishing Company, 1986).

²⁶ Pope John Paul II, *Familiaris consortio* (*The Role of the Christian Family in the Modern World*) (Boston: Daughters of St. Paul, 1981), p. 40.

²⁷ Ibid., p. 41.

²⁸ Edith Stein, *Essays on Woman*, trans. Freda Mary Oben (Washington, D.C.: ICS Publications, 1987), p. 47.

²⁹ Ibid., p. 48.

Mary Ellen Bork

COMMENT ON JANET SMITH'S "FEMINISM, MOTHERHOOD, AND THE CHURCH"

Feminists are engaged in an unparallelled assault on the institution of motherhood. They present Catholic women with a serious challenge: to seek a more profound understanding of Catholic teaching on woman and articulate it well to a culture vastly confused about women's roles. By reflecting on the faith view of woman expressed in sacred Scripture, papal documents, and in our own lives, we will persuade the women of our day that there is a better way. Janet Smith has done this with an ecumenical approach to feminists, pointing out where they agree with Christian teaching as well as their profound differences.

They applaud the Pope's defense of the equality of men and women but criticize his strong defense of motherhood as patriarchal. Janet defends the vocation of motherhood as a high Christian vocation, as the distinctively feminine vocation. She demonstrates how the Christian idea of motherhood does not fit into the feminist agenda because it is not a political concept. Feminists value an economic and political role in the public sphere more than a nurturing role in the private sphere. For them, mandatory motherhood is replaced by motherhood of choice. Feminists, by politicizing the subject of sexuality, block the possibility of a real discussion of Christian insights. Janet has accurately described their tenets as a "platform" with an agenda for action.

The four-part platform is a useful tool for summarizing the feminist position. Honest discussion is seriously hampered by the first plank, their own criterion of truth by which they decide what is "acceptable" or "unacceptable". Positive experiences of motherhood or relationships with men do not count. That reminds me of Molly Yard during our nomination ordeal who was asked to be available for the MacNeil Lehrer show. When they did not call her, she called them to say she was ready. They said they did not need her because the panel was full. She said it was important they have a woman. They said they did. She asked who it was. When she was told it was Carla Hills, then a prominent lawyer, she said, "But she's not a woman." Such a rigid and political notion of truth makes any appreciation of the Church's position on motherhood almost impossible.

The feminist goal is to liberate women from male oppression, which they see everywhere. That some women have suffered because of male misunderstanding is undoubtedly true. Some even suffer from male understanding. But that does not give a warrant for a transformation of the culture to achieve one group's liberation. Unfortunately, the ideology cannot seem to liberate without rejecting the feminine. One of feminism's most notable characteristics is a hostility to what is feminine. This is coupled with a rejection of what is natural in favor of an idea of human nature, and the nature of women, liberated from the bondage to gender. This vision of a "secret self", which, once released, will give the liberation they seek, fuels their agenda.

Maggie Gallagher in her book *Enemies of Eros* describes this secret self: "Underneath the layers of social conditioning lies a more genuine being, undistorted by gender, delightfully flexible, uninhibited, neither masculine nor feminine but in full possession of a divine, free personhood."[1] This better self is an individual who operates in perfect freedom without outside influences, choosing lifestyle, sexual orientation, goals, and personality traits. "If this better self is to be liberated then all hindrances must be sloughed off. Layers of artificial culture must be stripped off so we can be our real androgynous selves."[2] With this vision of the "secret self", they seek to replace any semblance of the understanding of woman presented by Scripture as created in complementarity with man to be wife, friend, and mother. The "secret self" is a "mask for expressions of personal preference".[3]

Feminists are rooted in a basically emotive view of the world and of history which distorts their theoretical perceptions.[4] By denying the feminine and actually attacking it they are acting out of false and essentially nihilistic ideas about who they are. They are working out their political agenda in the concrete, but their blueprint for liberation is not rooted in reality. Trying to impose antifeminine values on women to right a perceived wrong does not improve things. In the name of equality, we do not have to deny gender to find happiness.

The radical feminist position is in complete opposition to the traditional Christian view because it reduces the role of woman to economic and political competition with men. The Church sees the feminine vocation, not as defined by the economic and political spheres of life, nor as alienated from them, but as primarily a call to sacrificial love that is closely allied with the Christian vocation to love one another. The Pope calls for the promotion of woman but not without preserving the distinctively feminine gifts. That is simply not enough for most feminists. They do not see that dignity is rooted not in power but in integrity in following the God-given call of being created a woman. Their position seduces by promising a pseudosophisticated freedom, while the Christian position suffers from being seen as part of a set of accepted traditional values which we take for granted. A healthy note, as Janet points out, is seen in those feminists who break ranks and will not totally let go of traditional insights into the value of motherhood. This results in events like Connie Chung's announcing, not only to her husband but to the world as well, that she was going to take time off to have a baby.

Janet highlights the importance of the Church's teaching on sexuality which safeguards the sanctity of marriage and motherhood. This teaching supports the order created by God and redeemed by Christ. This creation reveals an order in which women are created sexually superior to men precisely because of their role as mothers. This superiority is not a feminist claim but an anthropological fact. Women are the ones who conceive and carry the child and experience the tumult of birth and suckling the infant. In the Christian view of human life "fathers work to shape the world so that mothers may do their work well."[5] If women start competing with them in the economic sphere, the male role in society will be devalued, leaving them stranded and feeling a lack of respect.

Catholicism is in a countercultural position with a culture that is slowly taking away all supports for the institution of the family as we know it. The two groups of people who suffer the most from the feminist sexual agenda are mothers and children, through divorce (one in every two marriages ends in divorce), contraception, sterilization, abortion, and surrogate motherhood. The ideology is so strong that it encourages a woman to act against her deepest instinct: for example, walking away from her twelve-week-old baby to go back to work or demanding a divorce even though she knows her children will suffer. The Pope rightly calls the question of clarifying the role of woman an urgent one.

The two key points where feminists differ with the teaching of the Church are their anthropology—they want androgyny—and their understanding of freedom as choice, not freedom as choice of the good. In their effort to be liberated, many feminists have abandoned women. The Church holds fast to her teaching that women's true liberation will come through a full appreciation of motherhood. Our effort now is to discern and resist the influence of these ideas in our lives, "renew our minds" with a deep spirituality, and speak out about this great truth to a society that needs the femininity it punishes in women.

Saint Augustine faced a similar situation. He said, quoting 1 Corinthians 11:19, "There must be many heresies, that they which are approved may be made manifest among you", in other words, that heresies do the Church a lot of good.

There are in the Holy Church innumerable men approved by God, but they do not become manifest among us so long as we are delighted with the darkness of our ignorance, and prefer to sleep rather than to behold the light of truth. So, many are awakened from sleep by the heretics, so that they may see God's light and be glad. Let us therefore use even heretics, not to approve their errors, but to assert the Catholic discipline against their wiles, and to become more vigilant and cautious, even if we cannot recall them to salvation.[6]

NOTES

[1] Maggie Gallagher, *The Enemies of Eros* (Chicago: Bonus Books, 1989), p. 132.
[2] Ibid., p. 135.
[3] Alasdair MacIntyre, *After Virtue: A Study in Moral Theology* (Notre Dame, Ind.: Notre Dame University Press, 1984), p. 19.
[4] Ibid.
[5] See above, Janet E. Smith, "Feminism, Motherhood, and the Church", p. 59.
[6] Saint Augustine, *On True Religion* (Chicago: Henry Regnery, 1959), p. 16.

Alice von Hildebrand

EDITH STEIN

The spiritual vitality of the Roman Catholic Church is strikingly manifested in the fact that she brings us an immediate remedy for every disease. It is truly providential that at a time when feminism is spreading like wildfire among laymen, and alas, also among priests and nuns, the Church has beatified Edith Stein—a woman—Jewish by birth, who obtained her Ph.D. in philosophy summa cum laude, converted to Roman Catholicism, became a Carmelite nun, and died in a German concentration camp.

I mean also to contrast her with another famous woman, Simone de Beauvoir, whose life had its own reversals and paradoxes: a born Catholic who "converted" to atheism, a feminist who devoted her life to Jean-Paul Sartre.

Edith Stein was born in Breslau on October 12, 1891, which happened, that year, to coincide with the great Jewish Day of Atonement. She was the last of eleven children, four of whom died at a very young age. Her mother was a deeply pious woman, whose life was marked by a strong moral sense and a deep reverence which she tried to inculcate in her children. There is little doubt that the mother—who was over forty years of age at Edith's birth—nurtured a particular affection for her youngest child, a child destined to lose her father when she was only two years old. Finding herself a widow, Augusta Stein was forced to take over the family business. She managed to combine intense professional work with her duties as mother. Moreover, she faithfully attended Jewish religious ceremonies and would fast on the days prescribed by the Law. Apparently,

Edith never suffered from her mother's professional activities. Augusta Stein's great heart made up in quality for the time she could not devote to her children.

Edith's outstanding talents were apparent at a very early age, and she vied with her older brothers and sisters in acquiring knowledge. From the very beginning of her education, she was collecting all the prizes and awards. She was remarkably disciplined, and had a very strong will. She thus brought to fruition all her talents through hard work, a noble ambition, and an ardent love for truth. She was also a remarkable linguist—a fact which enabled her to enlarge greatly her intellectual field. Her secondary schooling completed, she turned to the study of Latin, and, in a short time, she mastered the tongue of Cicero, not suspecting that this classical language was going to play a crucial role later in her life.

Can we say that Edith underwent a religious crisis during her adolescence? One thing is certain: she drifted away from the faith of her youth and became an agnostic, if not an atheist. For this reason, it is tempting to compare her to another famous woman, sixteen years her junior: Simone de Beauvoir, the French existentialist, the faithful disciple of Jean-Paul Sartre. The names of these two women will go down in history, but for very different reasons.

Simone de Beauvoir came from a comfortable French milieu. Her father was a typical French liberal of the twentieth century; her mother had been educated in a convent and was very pious, but, alas, due to her prudishness and the narrowness of some of her views, at the time of Simone's adolescence she inevitably triggered her willful daughter's violent opposition. Simone had only one younger sister, who soon became her rebellious accomplice and joined her in opposing the strait-laced religious education their mother was trying to impose upon them. While in her teens, Simone had clearly given up any form of belief or religious life, much to her mother's sorrow. Her meeting Jean-Paul Sartre at the Sorbonne when she was twenty-one years old sealed her atheism and gave her thought a direction to which, unfortunately, she remained faithful to the very end of her life.

In spite of the differences in background, it is fascinating to compare Edith Stein and Simone de Beauvoir. Both had received a religious education: Edith was raised an orthodox Jew; Simone, a Roman Catholic. Both were outstandingly gifted; both abandoned their faith at an early age; both received a degree in philosophy. But whereas Edith experienced a radical conversion and became an ardent Roman Catholic, Simone moved further and further away from what she interpreted as hypocritical conventions, or outdated beliefs. How are we to explain that these two women who, for a while, seemed to be running along parallel paths, ended their lives at antipodes?

A brief analysis of their respective attitudes when they lost their faith and their reasons for doing so will shed some light on this question. From the time of puberty on, Simone de Beauvoir's attitude was characterized by a systematic rebellion against her background, her education, and very particularly against her pious mother. Simone's father, while conservative in politics, was extremely liberal in his religious views. His daughter rejected his conservatism but endorsed his liberalism which she carried to its final consequences. A perusal of Simone de Beauvoir's memoirs[1] convinces one that "rebellion" constituted the very core of her attitude toward life and strongly colored both her behavior and her philosophy. She is the living embodiment of a religious and metaphysical defiance. She cannot help but show her disdain for faith, and especially for Roman Catholicism, even as she betrays an amazing ignorance of the doctrines of the Church. Strange as it may sound, this highly sophisticated woman, who was a brilliant student and had the reputation of having "a man's mind", basically remained immature, in both her views and conduct. No doubt, it is a typical symptom of puberty to rebel, to oppose, to reject authority, education, and tradition. It is a way of asserting one's independence and of proclaiming loudly that "one has come of age". But this is an attitude which normally wanes when a person reaches some authentic maturity. In Simone de Beauvoir, however, not only did it not diminish, but it remained the leitmotiv of her existence. Justified as she was in rejecting stifling conventions to which she had been forced to conform while under her parents' tutelage, she was certainly not justified in identifying all morality with conventions, simply because, in her milieu, conventions had been confused with morality. Her rejection of her past is totally "unselective" and indiscriminate and, for this reason, is marked by irrationality. She prided herself on being a liberated woman—a woman who had thrown overboard the ballast of traditional (that is, in her views, conventional) morality. In a spirit of sheer opposition, she endorsed immoral, nay, totally amoral views, thereby proving that she was too immature to distinguish wisely between conventions and authentic morality.

This puerile attitude (so often found among famous and successful intellectuals) also manifests itself in her irrational craving for what she calls "freedom". But freedom in her mouth, actually means a blind yielding to whims, moods, and subjective desires. The very first lines of her book, *La Force de l'Âge*, give us a key to her attitude. She tells us that she was inebriated by the fact that, having left her family, she could finally do what she pleased, when she pleased, because she pleased. Educators know that this wild craving to follow one's whims (caprices) is typical of the age of puberty. How marvelous it was for her to spend her days according to her moods, to go to whatever movie happened to strike her fancy, to read any book that happened to cross her path; how "liberating" to visit "boites" and bars and to smoke (however unskillfully). How inebriating to be one's own master and to owe everything to oneself!

Ironically, the immature person, then, feels particularly mature because she now rules her life and has neither need to ask for permission nor fear that she is being pressured.

Hand in hand with this childish trait, is Simone's rejection of any responsibility. She wants to live for herself; she acts very much as if others were just "pieces" on the chessboard of her cravings and desires.

How different was Edith Stein's attitude! She, too, had abandoned the faith of her youth, but she did so, not out of a spirit of rebellion, but because she had not found in it the spiritual nourishment for which she longed. The fact that she remained deeply reverent toward her mother proves this eloquently. Edith never rebelled for the sake of rebelling. She simply rejected what she could not believe in. Moreover, her rejection of Judaism did not lead her to abandon morality. Her mother's sound moral teaching was in no way affected by Edith's agnosticism. A remark she makes in her autobiography[2] is very enlightening. She tells us that had she known at that time the Roman Catholic teaching about love and marriage, she would have endorsed it unconditionally. Her attitude toward the sexual sphere was marked by reverence. For Simone de Beauvoir, on the contrary, marriage had become a bourgeois abomination, sexual morality was a tissue woven by hypocrisy, and she went from "prudishness" to shamelessness without any transition. While traversing this trajectory, she never encountered the virtue of purity, proving thereby that purity is not between these two extremes: it is above them. In fact, her allusions to the sexual sphere are characterized by a coarseness of language that makes one blush; she seems to feel a keen and perverse satisfaction in entering into unnecessary details in order to prove to herself again and again that sexual morality is nothing but a hollow web of stupid conventions. One gains the conviction that, in her fight for feminism, she has lost any trace of femininity. Sad to relate, she tailored her life on the principle of "free love".

Edith Stein never shunned responsibilities; once again, what an abyss yawns between her autobiography and the memoirs of Simone de Beauvoir! Edith always was "other-conscious", ready to help those in need, and aware that she was "her brother's keeper".

Conscious of her intellectual talents, proud of her intellectual achievements, Simone de Beauvoir's attitude toward life was marked by a tremendous self-assurance, tainted by arrogance and irreverence. No doubt, the young Edith was also self-assured; her brilliant scholastic successes had made her aware of her great talents. But she was neither arrogant nor irreverent. When she came to the University of Göttingen, she was animated by a sincere desire to learn from people who knew more than she and were wiser.

Even though Simone de Beauvoir often mentions the word "truth", one cannot evade the feeling that, in her mouth, it usually means whatever she and Sartre have endorsed. The fact that she disdainfully rejects "eternal verities" speaks volumes. Edith, on the other hand, was intent on discovering an objective truth, a truth—in Kierkegaard's words—for which she could live and die.

Grace presupposes nature, and the remarks just made should make it clear that huge rocks were blocking Simone de Beauvoir's path to both religion and authentic morality, whereas no such obstacles were to be found on Edith's road. She still had a long way to go, but she did not have to overcome the natural obstacles that her French counterpart had piled up through her rebelliousness. In spite of her flashes of brilliance and of her literary talents, much of de Beauvoir's works are marked by superficiality and a definite "will" not to bother herself with "useless" spiritual and religious questions, which she then discards with a wave of hand. At the same time, she is objectively so ignorant of the nature of authentic Roman Catholicism that she can make statements about faith that are not only preposterous but totally unscholarly—and what can be more damning in an "intellectual"? Her views are marked by a tremendous self-assurance and a note of arrogance which she seems to justify by the all-powerful argument: Sartre thinks so too; or still more frequently: "we" think such and such.

One thing is certain: Simone de Beauvoir is typically irreverent, and this irreverence bars her way to objective truth. The most grievous intellectual errors in the long history of thought are to be traced back, not to lack of intellectual talents, but to the moral vice that is irreverence. This explains why famous scholars and thinkers can make mistakes which are so primitive and so shallow that they would never be found in "simple" people who have not gained for themselves the reputation of being "geniuses" with the vocation to reinvent the universe.

Edith could have followed a similar path. But she was saved by her reverence. Her "atheism" was in no way related to basic irreverence, to amorality, or to subjectivism: this fact explains (apart from the all-crucial factor called "grace") why Edith and Simone will at one point follow paths leading in opposite directions. These two talented women became as different from each other as Kierkegaard differed from Nietzsche and my husband differed from Jean-Paul Sartre.

In his *Antimemoirs*, André Malraux relates that he once asked a priest, point-blank, what was the most instructive lesson he had learned in the confessional. With no hesitation, the priest answered: "There are no grown-up people." Few humans are able to leave the infantile stage, that is, to abandon childishness while becoming "childlike". Apart from the strenuous effort required for such an accomplishment, it calls for a full collaboration with grace. What is particularly amazing, however, is that maturity is more likely to be found in simple peasant women than in sophisticated intellectuals. Rousseau immediately comes to mind, and Simone de Beauvoir deserves to join him in the club of talented thinkers whose character still has all the marks of immaturity.

The combination of infantilism in character and sophistication in intellectual pursuits makes for an explosive situation: not only for others, who are bound to be severely affected by it, but also for the infantile person himself, for this basic defect will color not only his or her character but his or her accomplishments as well.

No doubt the young Edith Stein had her weaknesses; she certainly was self-assured, and she was easily critical of others. But the very fact that she recognized true greatness and superiority when she met it testifies to the fact that she remained opened to correction and improvement.

When she arrived in Göttingen in the spring of 1913, she had acquired a certain maturity. Her responses were not earmarked by opposition and irrationality; she knew how to control her whims, and she certainly did not refuse to shoulder responsibilities. It would still take time before she was to reach the full maturity of those who have become "like little children", that is to say, those who have conquered eternal youth, in their closeness to God who *"laetificat juventutem meam"*.

It is particularly interesting to examine carefully her inner attitude upon meeting both Husserl and Reinach. One senses that she approached these two men with the reverent longing of someone who seeks truth and hopes to find it. Much as she revered Edmund Husserl, however, it is clear—and all her friends knew this—that the man who impressed her most was Adolf Reinach, not only intellectually but also as a personality. Reinach was Husserl's assistant and was eight years her senior. He was universally recognized by his students as "the phenomenologist par excellence", the ideal teacher, and simultaneously the man who attracted and deserved friendship. What a world separates Reinach from Sartre! The saying is true indeed: "Tell me what you love, and I will tell you who you are." Simone de Beauvoir chose to devote her life to Jean-Paul Sartre. Edith Stein found in Reinach a man who, humanly speaking, was clearly her ideal. That he deserved the loving admiration she gave him will not be contested by anyone who knew him. Not only was he an outstanding thinker, but he too was animated by a passionate love for truth. To meet him was to meet someone characterized by intelligence, probity, straightforwardness, honesty, and goodness. These qualities that impregnated his whole personality were written on his face and reflected in his very words. In spite of his superb intellectual gifts, he was characterized by a great modesty, conscious of the awesomeness of truth and of the limitations of man's mind. He approached every question with a deep reverence, anxious not to impose his own "opinions" on his students. "Opinions" belong to the individual holding them, whereas truth belongs to no one, or, rather, it is open to everyone who seeks it with "purity of heart". But when Reinach knew he had conquered a truth, he could share his discovery with the convincing clarity and ardor typical of the great teacher. Quite apart from all these outstanding and appealing qualities, Reinach was also a Jew, and no doubt felt a great affinity with the reserved and brilliant young girl who had become his student.

In Göttingen, Edith found an ideal intellectual climate to develop her talents; it opened up for her completely new vistas. She had now found people who were intellectually her superiors, and she gratefully accepted their guidance. But these ideal circumstances, so propitious to fruitful intellectual advances, were not to last long. Some fifteen months after her arrival in Göttingen, Europe became engaged in the horrible and suicidal World War I, which ended Edith's studies with Reinach. An ardent German patriot, the latter immediately volunteered for the army despite the fact that he was already over thirty at the time and, moreover, being very nearsighted, was not likely to be recruited. As a matter of fact, in order to be accepted in the army, he had to engage the help of his younger brother, Heinrich, who was an officer. After a brief period of training, he was sent to the Belgian front where, some three years later, he was killed in action.

Animated by the same patriotic feelings as Reinach (for most Jews were ardent German patriots), Edith volunteered to do Red Cross work, and for several months she devoted herself to the wounded and the sick with her whole heart and all her loving intelligence. Edith proved to be outstandingly talented as a nurse. The months she spent in a military hospital in Austria unveil for us an aspect of Edith's personality which the brilliance of her intellectual accomplishments tended to obscure: her deep femininity. The services she so lovingly performed for the sick and wounded, under circumstances which were extremely difficult, prove how removed she was from the egotism so apparent in Simone de Beauvoir (whose main preoccupations during World War II were survival and the furthering of Sartre's plays). Edith joyfully shouldered responsibilities. She never hesitated to give herself to others when she was called upon to do so. Nursing the sick exposed her to the danger of contagion, even though she wisely took the necessary precautions to protect herself from infection. But her loving concern was focused on the patients, not herself.

Several times, she had the joy of receiving a brief message from Reinach, the man for whom she nurtured such loving admiration. She had the joy of seeing him once more when he came back to Göttingen on a brief furlough during the Christmas holiday of 1916.

In the meantime, however, he had converted to Protestantism. Perhaps I may be permitted to sketch briefly the story of his conversion. It was clear to all who knew him that Reinach was, like Daniel, "a man of longing" (Saint Bonaventure). That his passionate love for truth should lead him to raise religious questions was inevitable. Both he and his wife became attracted to Christianity. While he was at the front reading the *Confessions* of Saint Augustine and the Benedictine Schott Missal, which my husband (himself a young convert) had sent him, his wife, Anna, made the acquaintance of a Protestant clergyman, to whom she confided her interest in Christianity. When her husband came home on a furlough, she suggested to him that both of them should be immediately baptized. To this, Adolf objected that even though he had become convinced of the divinity of Christ, he had no time to examine the basic differences between Roman Catholicism and Protestantism, and for this reason would rather postpone baptism; he needed time to discover where the full truth was to be found.

Anna retorted that this was precisely something that could be examined later on, that the Protestant minister was not that exacting and was willing to baptize them in spite of this intellectual reservation. The main thing was to receive the grace of baptism. Adolf yielded to his wife's wishes, and they both were baptized. Soon afterward, Reinach was killed.

His wife's sorrow was immense. They had been married for just over five years. Reinach's name was but one on a long and tragic list of most promising young men who were sacrificed during this brutal conflict. Friends were thunderstruck; it seemed to them inconceivable that such a noble and talented human being, who had been such a beacon in their lives, should have left this earth, struck by a bullet in the eye. The meaningless of the murderous conflict that was tearing Europe apart came blaringly to the fore.

My husband was heartbroken; he had lost not only a revered teacher but a very dear friend as well. We can assume that Edith was immediately informed of this terrible event, but, with her usual reserve, she kept her sorrow hidden in her heart. Knowing of Reinach's conversion to Protestantism, she now had the opportunity of discovering the strength that Adolf's widow derived from her new faith. For Edith, too, the loss was immense; apart from his human goodness which had touched her heart, Reinach had been her guide and mentor. He had been a light in her life, and this light was now forever extinguished. Devoting herself to putting Reinach's papers in order, Edith probably was the closest witness of Anna's struggle with widowhood.

When Reinach's body was brought to Göttingen in December 1917, his father asked my husband to say a few words at the tomb. It was in these tragic circumstances that Dietrich von Hildebrand made the acquaintance of Edith Stein. He had, of course, heard about her. Also she knew of him, and she mentions his name several times in her autobiography. Since both had been shattered by this irreparable loss, my husband assumed that their common sorrow would create a deep bond between them. But he found her to be so closed up, so reserved that, alas, no deep contact could develop between them.

Edith had remained close to Hedwig Conrad Martius (another brilliant student of both Husserl and Reinach) whose religious background was Protestant. While staying at the latter's farm late in 1921, one evening when her friend and her friend's husband were absent, Edith happened to find the autobiography of Saint Teresa of Avila. She was so struck by the beauty and depth of this work that she spent the whole night reading it.

Upon closing the book, Edith had gained the absolute and unshakeable conviction that she had found not only truth, but, indeed, the Truth. She got herself a missal and instructed herself in the Faith. When, soon afterward, she turned to a Catholic priest and asked to be baptized, he found, to his surprise, that she had a very deep knowledge of Catholicism and needed no further instruction. She was baptized on January 1, 1922. She was then thirty years old.

Mrs. Batzdorff, Edith Stein's niece, had an article about her aunt published in the *New York Times Magazine* in 1987 (at the time of Edith Stein's beatification). In this article, Mrs. Batzdorff tries to give a psychological explanation for her aunt's conversion to Roman Catholicism. She reasons that several professors and fellow students at Göttingen had abandoned Judaism to become Christians, mostly for political reasons. She admits, however, that this was definitely not the case with her aunt. She concludes that Edith, therefore, found herself in a psychological climate favoring conversion to Christianity.

It is true that Husserl had become Protestant, but he was a low-key, liberal Protestant, who carefully refrained from examining religious questions. His approach was exclusively dictated by purely rational interests. It is true that Edith had a profound admiration for this talented thinker. But we have no reason to assume that he exercised any sort of religious influence on her. Adolf Reinach was the one person whose judgment was likely to have an immense weight with her. But Edith converted to Roman Catholicism, not to Protestantism.

The only Catholic that Edith met while studying at Göttingen was Max Scheler, who was, in fact, a fallen-away Catholic. He briefly came back to the Church in 1916, when Edith was no longer in Göttingen. It is clear from her autobiography that Edith immediately sensed Scheler's genius, and that, thanks to his teaching, she opened up to certain metaphysical and religious problems which had remained foreign to her. It is equally clear, however, that Scheler's brilliant but erratic personality did not mark her in any profound sense.

At the time in question, the only two persons connected with Göttingen University who had become ardent Roman Catholics were my husband and his closest friend and collaborator, Siegfried Hamburger. However, my husband had left Göttingen in 1912, a year before Edith came to that famous university, and Hamburger converted in 1914, just at the beginning of the First World War. The latter was also Jewish and, like Edith, came from eastern Germany, Kattowitz. Edith knew him, for Hamburger was still in Göttingen when she came in 1913, but since he was as shy and reserved as she was, and since his conversion took place after he had left Göttingen for good, it truly seems inappropriate to speak of any Catholic influence exercised on Edith while she was at Göttingen. This small German town was no hotbed of Roman Catholicism.

Mrs. Batzdorff also laments over the fact that her aunt caused untold sufferings to her family, especially to her elderly mother. Not a word is said about Edith's own sufferings.

When asked about her conversion, Edith is supposed to have answered: "My secret belongs to me." It is definitely not our intention to probe into the mystery of Edith's soul. Indeed, there is a secret cell in the human soul where God alone can penetrate, and it would be irreverent to force entry into this mysterious region to which God alone has the solitary key.

Yet, it seems certain that the reading of Saint Teresa's autobiography opened up for Edith a new world: the world of the supernatural. Prior to this, she had been concerned about truth, scholarship, beauty, friendship, family ties: all noble but purely natural values. But what she discovered during that night, which was to be to her brighter than day, was another world, another melody, another song, so much more sublime, so much more lofty, revealing harmonies that definitely could not come from this earth in spite of all its greatness and beauty. This overwhelming discovery of a new reality has been made by many famous converts. It is a discovery that my own husband made when he read the life of Saint Francis of Assisi and was enraptured by the new world that became visible to him through this most Christlike of saints.

How is one to express this radiance of this newly found country to those who have never experienced it? How is one to describe the sun to those who have always lived by candlelight? Plato must have had some inkling of this when, in book VII of the *Republic*, he tells us about the philosopher who, leaving the dark cave, suddenly discovers the sun. With her keen and open mind, Edith Stein must have sensed that all the nobility of natural morality (which meant so much in her life) suddenly paled when compared to the revelation of Christian charity and humility. Saint Augustine tells us that he had found some admirable virtues among pagans, but that never, absolutely never, had he found these two sublime virtues, which presuppose revelation and divine grace in order to be realized in the frail vessel of man's imperfection. Edith must have perceived that charity infinitely transcends justice, and, at the same time, fulfills the latter in a way in which it cannot be fulfilled on a merely natural plane. She must have tasted the sweetness of Divine Mercy that calls the sinner to loving repentance. She must have understood something of Christ's holy madness of love, choosing humiliation, suffering, agonizing pains and death for the sake of saving sinful humanity from God's wrath. Saint Teresa's ardent love for her fellow men must have illumined for Edith the teaching of Christ that we should love our enemies, pray for those who persecute us, and offer ourselves as victims to save them from eternal damnation. What a night it must have been for her when, all of a sudden, she was given to see that Truth is a Person, the infinitely Holy One, and that, therefore, Truth is not only to be revered, but, in fact, can and should be loved as only a person can be loved. Indeed, in Christ she found not only the fulfillment of all intellectual longing— for he is the Truth—but also the object that deserved the full giving of her heart, of her mind, of herself. Not only was her mind illumined, her heart was simultaneously conquered. And this Divine Being, the object of Saint Teresa's adoration, was a Jew, one of her race, the fulfillment of the promise given to the chosen people, the Messiah. Can we not assume that this inebriating night revealed to Edith the privilege of belonging to the Jewish race? She had abandoned the Jewish faith and become "liberal" in her views; she had probably rejected the idea of a chosen people, to whom God had confided a unique message: his personal revelation. All of a sudden, to her, the "Apostate Jew", the grace was given to understand the true nature of Judaism and the extraordinary dignity of a race that has received the awesome honor of giving birth to the King of the universe. And she, Edith, had received the privilege of belonging to that very race. Hand in hand with this revelation, she must have experienced an immense sorrow. Her heart must have bled upon realizing that her own people, her own dear family, were blind to the overwhelming gift they had received in Christ. Was it not her mission to pray that they may one day share with her the unmerited gift she had received?

In a flash, she must have intuited the profound meaning of suffering and the intimate connection existing between the mystery of suffering and salvation. Indeed, Christ has said: "There is no greater love than to give one's life for one's friends." And this is precisely what he—the Man of Sorrows preannounced by Isaiah—had done in order to save sinful humanity from eternal damnation. If she could not convince her loved ones, was she not called upon to suffer for them?

Edith was a genuinely feminine woman, and thus, her mind worked best when it was animated by her heart. Her heart had now been wounded by the Divine Love, that all-embracing love which had led Saint Teresa of Avila to exclaim: "*Aut pati aut mori*" (Let me suffer, or let me die). This was to have consequences for Edith which would mark her life from 1922 until her death in 1942. From now on, she was going to give her absolute priority to love. Until now, she had concentrated all her efforts exclusively on the intellectual pursuit of rational truth. It must have given her no small satisfaction to feel that she could compete intellectually with any gifted man (see her autobiography). Even a superficial perusal of this book allows us to see with what passionate devotion she had given herself to the task of acquiring knowledge. She would work for hours on end, until late in the night; in this she was like Simone de Beauvoir, often studying to the point of exhaustion. Her knowledge and scholarship were amazing—apart from the months she spent in an Austrian military hospital, Edith had immersed herself in her arduous studies until she was twenty-five. Her scholarship was as deep as it was rigorous.

From now on, Edith's heart was going to fecundate her mind; the two would no longer be separated. This resolve will give to her work a warmth which can never be found in purely abstract intellectual treatises. Her new vision did not lead Edith to abandon philosophy; but, great and respectable as philosophical pursuit was, it was now superseded by a greater love. She had faith, and this faith was to be lived, not by turning to more books and more studies, but by praying, nay, by adoring. Once again, it is a very feminine trait that Edith immediately adopted: her newly won faith had to become a life, had to be incarnated in her very self, had to become her very flesh and blood. She was no longer content with knowing; she wanted to love, for to love is to live truly and fully.

Like my husband, Edith never lost her love for the noblest of human sciences: philosophy. She always remained conscious of the great gift she had received in her philosophical training that pointed her so powerfully toward an objective truth, gloriously independent of man's mind, but nevertheless accessible to his mind. And yet, philosophy was now dethroned for her, that is to say, it was replaced by a nobler, higher reality which had been revealed to her through Saint Teresa. And it was the full possession of this higher reality for which Edith now longed with all her heart. She must have intuited that the new path to which she was now so clearly called, was that of the Cross—the blessed Cross which bore the Savior of the world.

Let me, once again, mention Edith's femininity in this regard. Apart from her experiences as a nurse this trait had been, as we have seen, somewhat veiled, but now it came to full bloom. Her own gifts had tempted Edith to endorse the philosophy of feminism. In her autobiography, she relates that once she had a discussion with her sister Erna and a friend as to whether a woman should sacrifice her career for husband and child. Edith definitely rejected the idea and protested that she would never dream of giving up her intellectual pursuits, for any reason whatever. Her sister and her friend, on the contrary, pleaded in favor of the family. In one of those strange twists of history, it turned out that both Erna and her friend married but kept their careers, whereas Edith chose to sacrifice everything—degrees, honors, success, research, publication—for the sake of a total gift to Christ—the King of the Jews.

From this moment on, her femininity blossomed like a gentle flower, watered by the morning dew. It also molded anew her face which up to now had something severe, almost forbidding about it. It had displayed both strength and a fierce reserve. If we compare her early photos with those taken after Edith had donned the Carmelite habit, we notice a striking physical change. Friends who visited her in the Carmel say that at the time of her vesture, her face was rejuvenated. It was stamped with a gentleness and sweetness heretofore unknown to them.

We might think that once Edith had become a believer, her great talents would remain buried or would wither. But this would be a great error. No one can beat God's generosity, and we shall see that her renunciation of earthly wisdom was compensated by a higher wisdom which became more and more apparent as she came closer to her crucifixion in Auschwitz. Edith now had Saint Teresa as a model, and no doubt, this great mystic led her to the holiest of all women, Mary, the sweet flower of Jesse, the loveliest blossom of the Jewish race.

Far be it from me to claim that all this had become crystal clear to Edith during this one night of grace. But the seeds certainly had all been planted, and they would blossom in due season.

Finally, we may assume that, hand in hand with her blessed

conviction that she had found the fullness of truth, came the premonition to Edith that this precious pearl would bring with it a crushing cross: the rejection of her family. She had heard the glorious call addressed to the Chosen People, and she responded with all her heart. But in that very moment, she was bound to realize that neither her beloved mother nor her six siblings would understand the overwhelming experience that she had had. They would interpret her conversion to Roman Catholicism as a form of betrayal. This form of betrayal was not much linked to Nazism, which, in 1922, was nothing more than a small (however poisonous) seed. But Edith knew, through her education, how Jews interpret conversions, how they feel betrayed when one of their own race abandons their tradition. This feeling, of course, is experienced by the Orthodox Jews, but surprisingly enough it is shared equally by those who have become totally liberal in their views, but whose abandonment of religion is usually compensated by a virulent nationalism (e.g., Zionism).

Edith understood that to become a Christian means not only to accept the cross, but also to embrace it lovingly, sustained by the faith that suffering out of love, and suffering coupled with prayer, has the power to open the eyes of the privileged people who had given birth to the Savior of the world and yet had failed, as a race, to recognize him. Jesus himself had uttered the solemn words: "He who would follow me must carry his cross; he who does not hate father and mother for my sake is not worthy of me." No long meditation is needed to understand the implication of these words. With her great intelligence and sensitivity, now refined by grace, Edith must have perceived with terrible acuity the human consequences of this night of grace. She was to offer herself as a sacrifice for her loved ones, and also for the Jewish race.

All of us are tempted to select our own cross and to complain that the one God chooses for us is the most crushing. Edith knew intuitively that God had chosen for her the one cross that she dreaded: to be rejected by her mother, the person to whom she owed so much, who had surrounded her with the most selfless love. According to Jewish Law it is the mother's blood that determines whether or not a child is born a Jew. Thus, it was through her mother that Edith had entered the Jewish race. Although the rejection and the misunderstanding of her siblings was extremely painful to her, none of them was so close to her, or so dear to her heart, as was her noble, venerable mother. She knew now that the day would come when she must tell her mother that she had received baptism and had entered the Roman Catholic Church. After this, the break was inevitable.

In Verdi's opera, *La Traviata*, Violetta sings an aria in which the words "*croce, delizia*" (cross and ecstasy) follow each other. On the supernatural plane, Edith must have experienced something similar: enraptured by her newly won faith, she simultaneously felt the weight of the cross on her shoulder.

Her premonition was all too accurate. Edith received the sacrament of baptism shortly after her night of grace. She knew she had an obligation to inform her mother that she was now a member of the Roman Catholic Church. She expected violent reproaches, perhaps even abuses. But her mother's response was still more devastating: Augusta Stein cried. And her tears must have burned in Edith's heart. How dreadful for a daughter to see her mother cry! But Edith's sorrow was doubled by the fact that she was the one who, in her mother's eyes, had caused the tears to flow. She thus had all the pain that guilt causes even though she knew herself to be guiltless. She was already a victim of her love for the Crucified.

But *jacta est alea*—the die had been cast—she had done what she had to do. She would gladly have agreed to carry her mother's suffering hidden in her own breast; but her mother, as it were, suffered alone, unwilling and perhaps unable to be consoled. The keenness of Edith's sorrow was increased by the fact that had her mother's eyes been opened, as her own eyes now were, the very thing that made her cry would have become a source of jubilation.

This happened in 1922; Edith Stein had still twenty more years to live before her spiritual crucifixion at Auschwitz would take place. It seems to me that these twenty years are nothing but the unfolding of the seed planted in her generous soul late in 1921. Now the love of God and of neighbor reigned supreme in her heart. No doubt there was still a steep ascent ahead of her, but, basically, the way was now clear for a total self-surrender, which found its completion when she entered the Carmel of Cologne in October 1933.

In finding Christ, Edith Stein had found the precious pearl in exchange for which a merchant sells all he has. As we have seen, her love for philosophy was superseded by a greater love: a love for him who said, "I am the Truth." But in loving Christ more, Edith—as we have seen—did not lose her love for philosophy. Indeed, as my husband was so fond of repeating, we love an object best when we give it proper place in the hierarchy of values. It was not only desirable, therefore, but also inevitable that Edith should wish to confront her philosophical training with the teaching of Thomas Aquinas, a philosopher, but also a great Catholic saint. She was encouraged to translate into German the latter's work *De Veritate*. While teaching full-time at a Dominican school in Speier and spending long hours in front of the Blessed Sacrament, she gave herself to this difficult task. Much as Saint Thomas' approach differed from the training that she had received in Göttingen, there was one crucial bond that united the two philosophies: the conviction that truth was objective, royally independent of the human mind, and yet rationally accessible to that mind. Edith was enriched by this confrontation. On the other hand, her translation and the commentaries she inserted benefited greatly from her "phenomenological" approach, marked by an ardent desire to eliminate the intellectual prejudices which so often block our path to truth.

No doubt, Edith was more than qualified to be on the graduate faculty of a university. There is something ludicrous in the fact that such a brilliant mind should spend years of her life teaching in a German high school. But at that time, university posts were not easily accessible to women. Edith—the feminist of yore—bore this disappointment with fortitude. Far from falling into the resentment and bitterness which characterize so many feminists today, she chose to devote herself to the task assigned to her with all her talents and all her heart. Why should she—the brilliant student of Husserl who got her doctorate *summa cum laude*—resent being overlooked, when her King and Savior was flouted, rejected, ridiculed, and crucified? In fact, this unfair treatment challenged her to do some in-depth work on feminism, to shed light on the true vocation of women. She found her inspiration in Mary, the new Mother she had acquired after being rejected by her beloved earthly mother. We cannot here, because of the constraints of time, elaborate on the deep and fruitful insights that she developed in her work dedicated to femininity, which found its public expression in a brilliant lecture that she gave at Salzburg in 1932 (Hochschulwochen).

The wound in Edith's heart caused by her mother's response to her conversion remained. In spite of all her loving efforts, nothing would assuage the bitterness which was festering in Augusta Stein's heart. As this bitterness increased, so did Edith's attraction to the Carmel. At first, her spiritual director had discouraged her from entering, convinced as he was that she had an important mission to fulfill in this world. But when, after obtaining a better position in Münster, she was shortly forced to resign because of her race, the way to the convent was opened to her. She entered in October 1933, less than nine months after Hitler had become Chancellor of Germany. This decision was, for her elderly mother, the last straw. From now on, her daughter was "dead" to her. Her daughter's heart bled for her; is it surprising that her last work should be entitled: *The Science of the Cross*?

One must sympathize with Augusta Stein, convinced as she was that her daughter had betrayed her own family and her own people. This was echoed by all her children, with the exception of one sister, Rosa, who was herself attracted to the

Faith, but waited until her mother's death to fulfill her wish to enter the Church. Even though all of her siblings had ceased to be believing Jews, all but Rosa were unanimous in their condemnation of Edith's decision.

Let me here raise a question about Augusta Stein, who had remained a most faithful Jew down to her very death in 1936. (She was spared the ultimate sorrow of being thrown into a concentration camp—those places of horror that were to see the annihilation of four of her children). The question is this: How did it happen that she, who knew the Jewish Scriptures and accepted it as God's word, should have overlooked the message contained for her in the heartrending story of Abraham? The Father of Faith, as he is called, was asked to sacrifice his only child, Isaac, the son of the promise, so as to prove that God was first and foremost in his heart. The story of Augusta Stein and of her youngest daughter is the story of Abraham, but in reverse. For here it is the child, Edith, who is asked to "sacrifice" her mother to prove her ultimate self-surrender to God. As a new Abraham, Edith was forced to give her beloved mother the impression that she no longer cared for her, as she raised the sword of Christ's "divisiveness" to "sacrifice" a life dearer to her than her own. But if Augusta Stein failed to meditate on this sublime and upsetting story, Edith did not fail. She must have understood that God was calling her to this ultimate sacrifice. Following our Lady of Mount Carmel, she spoke her full *fiat*, trusting that God in his infinite goodness and mercy would accept the sacrifice of her bleeding heart, in order to lead Israel to the King of the Jews. May we hope that God, in his infinite goodness and mercy, heard her prayer, and that at the awesome moment of death, he granted to the noble Augusta Stein the grace to recognize Christ as her King. Thus would Edith, who had received physical life from her mother, pay her back by becoming her spiritual mother, the one who obtained for her the grace of adoring Christ, the King of the Jews.

NOTES

[1] *Memoirs of a Dutiful Daughter* (New York: Harper and Row, 1974).
[2] *Life in a Jewish Family* (unfinished autobiographical account), ed. Dr. L. Gelber and Romaeus Leuren, O.C.D., trans. Josephine Koeppel, O.C.D., in the *Collected Works of Edith Stein*, 1 (Washington, D.C.: ICS Publications, 1986).

Anne Roche Muggeridge

COMMENT ON ALICE VON HILDEBRAND'S "EDITH STEIN"

I thank Dr. von Hildebrand for her beautiful paper. I was particularly struck by her comparison of Edith Stein with Simone de Beauvoir, the most influential and destructive feminist of our time. At first, I wondered if Dr. von Hildebrand's purpose was to contrast two kinds of feminism, what some might consider Edith Stein's constructive kind with Simone de Beauvoir's destructive brand. When later in her paper, however, she described Edith Stein's radical break with her early preconversion feminism, I decided that Dr. von Hildebrand is not part of the current misguided attempt within orthodox Catholic circles to baptize feminism.

One can understand why such an attempt is being made. Feminist ideology is now so pervasive and so powerful that even elements of the teaching Church have been seduced by its arguments, or have persuaded themselves that some sort of rapprochement is politically necessary. One recent depressing example is the U.S. Bishops' desperately confused pastoral letter on women. Let us pray to Blessed Edith Stein that it dies aborning. Rome and loyal bishops keep wistfully looking for a *good* feminism. At the special U.S. Bishops' Rome Summit, March 1989, Cardinal O'Connor blasted what he called "radical feminism", while Cardinal Law called for a "Christian feminism" which, he said, "is not only important but necessary". Rome and the bishops are whistling in the dark. There is no such thing as a good, a benign, feminism. *All* feminism is *radical*. Feminism is by far the most radical of the theologies of liberation, the one that strikes deepest at the roots of religion and society. There cannot be a "Catholic feminism" any more than there can be a "Catholic atheism". It is a contradiction in terms. Catholicism is transcendental and incarnational; feminism is secularist and anti-incarnational. Feminists are at war with God the Father. They mean to tear down Catholic cosmology. The Church's teachers shouldn't be flirting with them.

Dr. von Hildebrand's comparison of the lives of Edith Stein and Simone de Beauvoir functions as a modern parable, illuminating an important modern truth: Edith Stein stopped being a feminist *because she became a Catholic*; Simone de Beauvoir became a feminist *because she stopped being a Catholic*. Catholicism and feminism are intrinsically incompatible. That truth was obvious to everyone at the time Edith Stein joined the Catholic Church. It is not so clear now, when Catholicism is enduring a time of profound confusion about all its old certainties.

After Edith Stein became a Catholic, she thought with the mind of the Church, which meant that she stopped thinking in terms of the *rights* of women and wrote instead of the *separate vocation* of women according to nature and grace. Her own philosophical discipline, phenomenology, led her to Saint Thomas Aquinas. She developed her thinking on woman's nature and vocation from Aquinas' teaching that the soul is the formative principle of the body—*anima corporis forma*. Human nature has two species, male and female. The differences between the bodies of men and women indicate corresponding differences in spirituality and calling. The collaboration between husband and wife is characterized both by unity and particularity. Just as a woman's body is designed for mothering and nourishing, so a woman's soul and mind will be drawn to work demanding spiritual maternity, even if she never bears a child.

Stein's distinction between the masculine and feminine in human nature is anathema to modern feminism, which relentlessly insists that human nature is androgynous. However, her work now informs much of what comes from the Vatican on the vocation of women. I don't know whether her influence on Pope John Paul II is firsthand, but the Pope, also a phenomenologist, uses language and concepts strikingly close to those of Edith Stein, in his own original theology of the body, in his 1988 apostolic letter *Mulieris dignitatem* (*On the Dignity and Vocation of Women*) and in the sections of the *Rights and Role of Women* in *Familiaris consortio*, his exhortation following on the 1980 Synod on the family.

One further point: I understand why some people see Edith Stein as a possible benign feminist alternative. There are in her work certain unexamined feminist positions left over from her atheist years. One example must suffice: the old feminist dogma that *every* masculine occupation must be open to women occurs several times in her work and is faithfully echoed in papal and episcopal statements on the vocation of women. If she had lived longer, might she have reconsidered this and other unqualified positions? Would she, for instance, insist that the giver and nurturer of life be allowed to become a combat soldier? Also, in dealing with women's professions, her own single professional state led her to propose unrealistic and unworkable options to married professional women. She did not live to reexamine these positions. She was dealing with abstract theories, not with concrete situations.

There are very serious questions of *justice* at stake in the whole question of the participation of married women with children in demanding professions. Edith Stein said, for example (and I agree with her): "We should accept as normal that the married woman is restricted to domestic life at a time when her household duties exact her total energies." She also said, unarguably for a Catholic, that a woman must "sacrifice her profession to her vocation". This sounds very nice in theory, but it is terribly difficult to put into practice. We must remember that when the choice came for her, she laid down her beloved profession of teaching at once and embraced her true vocation.

It is not enough if we reject feminism in theory yet, in effect, practice it toward our families and professions.

But which of us would care to stand by all our former dogmatic pronouncements? Edith Stein is not a feminist. I offer as proof, if it's needed, the one exception she allowed to her dogma that all masculine occupations should be legally open to women. Thinking with her beloved Catholic Church, she accepted that the priesthood was closed to women by Catholic Tradition, even though she thought that the admission of women could not be dogmatically forbidden. For Blessed Edith Stein, Catholic Faith and feminist ideology were truly incompatible.

Mary Hayden

LOVE: THE CENTER OF THE CHRISTIAN LIFE

Introduction[1]

Cynics, sceptics, sadomasochists, cowards, and the selfish with a Christian bent have predictable responses to hearing that love is the center of the Christian life. The cynics think: "Sure, love may be the Christian center, but it cannot put food on my table. The world is too tough to rely on such saccharine sentiment." Sadomasochists smile: they think such love brings new opportunities for being a doormat and making others suffer from their mistreatment. The selfish shudder and then repress their conscience by an egocentric interpretation of what God and others can do for them. Cowards groan and slink away from their faith; Christian love leads to that scary place of one's own Calvary. After all, Christ commanded us to love others as he has loved us (Jn 15:12).

Are they right? Does Christian love make us incapable of dealing with the world except as doormats? Is suffering the essence of loving as Christ?

If so, how could the Christian God say (Jn 10:10): "I have come so that they might have life and have it more abundantly"? If so, then the angels at Bethlehem were ironical when they proclaimed: Rejoice, a Savior has been born (Lk 2:10–11). Rejoice? If the cynics, sadomasochists, and cowards are correct, they should have proclaimed: "Weep, oh, you poor mortals. Your days of glory and fun are over. Now you are delivered into the realm of pain and suffering. A realm where love sheds its peace and its joy and no longer brings human fulfillment."

Our choice is this: either Christian love brings humans into greater fulfillment, peace, and joy, *or* it lowers us into hell. Either grace perfects nature, or nature is tortured by grace.

Some choice—eh? The alternative we choose depends upon how we see God: Is God a father unlike our loving earthly fathers, who want us to be happy? Is it possible for an all-good God to design nature to be at war with grace? To make natural love opposed to Christian charity?

Saint Thomas Aquinas, the preeminent Catholic philosopher and theologian answers: No![2] He argues that one of the first functions of grace is to heal human nature (wounded by original sin) in such a way that we can become that which we were created to be.[3] God created humans to be fulfilled and happy through love.

But we don't live this way. Countering our faith in God's love are the doubts of cynics, the perversions of sadomasochists, the egocentricity of the selfish, and the fears of cowards. These impediments to love shall be examined below, beginning with fear.

Fear

Everyone fears suffering: even Christ prayed that he need not drink of the cup of suffering (Mt 26:39). Yet, his willingness to do his Father's will led to immersion in the cup of Calvary. Hence, our fears that his will leads to a personal Calvary are well-founded. But they are not to control us. Does the well-grounded fear of labor pains prevent a mother from giving birth? Why not? Her love of the child outweighs any suffering. Indeed, her love endures through pain and culminates in "joy that a child has been born into the world" (Jn 16:21). Note well: love conquers fear, and labor pains are not confined to Christian women.

No human can escape suffering. For suffering involves experiencing evil;[4] and it bears witness to our fallen condition.[5] For evil came into this world of ours through the sin of our first parents. Accordingly, pain and suffering are the lot of every human—Christian or not. This means that cowards who shrink from their faith in the hope that they can escape suffering are mistaken. Lack of courage does not dissolve problems or eliminate pain.[6] Neither does love. But love is still the proper antidote to fear: "Love casts out fear" (1 Jn 4:18). And so, to abandon faith in the love of God is to abandon hope for overcoming fear and coping with the suffering intrinsic to the human condition. Suffering forces a choice: "You can become hateful and bitter . . . or you can grow holy and Christ-like."[7] Our option: facing our suffering and following Christ's teaching ". . . to do good by one's suffering and to do good to those who suffer."[8] Such good cannot be done without picking up our cross daily and following Christ (Lk 9:23).

Following Christ may not eliminate the pain, but it can prevent immersion in the misery that comes from thinking that suffering is meaningless. For when we unite our suffering to Christ, we unite it to Calvary—and the world's salvation.[9] To accept our suffering and to dedicate it to redemption renders it a sacrifice. "To sacrifice something", Evely writes, "is to make it sacred, to make it God's, to make it love."[10] Only through love is suffering made bearable: "Love bears all things, believes all things, hopes all things, endures all things" (1 Cor 13:7). Indeed, John Paul II writes:

> In the messianic program of Christ, which is at the same time the program of the kingdom of God, suffering is present in the world in order to release love, in order to give birth to works of love toward neighbors, in order to transform the whole of human civilization into a "civilization of love". In this love the salvific meaning of suffering is completely accomplished and reaches its definitive dimension.[11]

For the love that Christ bore us, it is our task to build this civilization of love. As it is said in 1 John 4:10–12, "In this is love: not that we have loved God, but that he loved us and sent his Son as expiation for our sins. Beloved, if God so loved us, we also must love one another. . . . Yet if we love one another, God remains in us, and his love is brought to perfection in us." Accordingly, the Christian understanding of suffering follows this sequence: evil, suffering, God's merciful love, Calvary, salvation, personal dedication, civilization of love.

Now love not only enables suffering to take on its salvific meaning, but it also enables one to find ". . . in his suffering interior peace and even spiritual joy. Saint Paul speaks of such joy in the Letter to the Colossians."[12] This joy within suffering arises not from pain but from its salvific purpose and from love of one's brothers and sisters in Christ. After all, in Hebrews 12:2, it is written that ". . . Jesus, . . . for the joy set before him, endured a cross". Great love brings great endurance.

This is the reality of suffering: it stems from evil, but it is conquered by love. Indeed, without this Christian perspective, suffering is merely a burden. A burden so great that it seems to some a definitive denial of the goodness and/or the existence of God. The very plausibility of this denial arises because we have lost awareness of sin's ugly reality, and the immensity of what was lost in Eden:[13] namely, that we had died in our transgressions. If we were truly aware, then one wholly good person would suffice to prove God's existence and goodness.[14] For without a loving God, no one could transcend the Fall's quagmire of fear, doubt, perversions, selfishness, and suffering. Make no mistake, Christ is our Savior: our burdens he lightens; our prayers he answers. No longer can human dignity be lost through suffering.[15] Whatever the pain, he has been there. He knows. He cares. And if asked, he will give the power to endure and to make his triumph ours. Trust is the key. He trusts us not to crumble into despair. And, we must trust him that our suffering is not beyond our strength (1 Cor 10:13), that he is working for our good[16]—even when we cannot see it.

Thus, in this fallen world, there is no escape from a cross: evil touches everyone. Yet there is a transcendence by accepting suffering for Love's sake. Thereby we are enabled to deal with whatever crosses us through the divine perspective of redemption.[17] Because God first loved us with a never-ending love and loved us through death to the Resurrection, we can bear any trouble, any pain by uniting it to his Cross. As Louis Evely writes: "There is only one means to endure our suffering and that is to understand His, to hook ours onto His, to remember that ours is His. 'I am glorified in them' (Jn 17:10)."[18] Transcendence is through uniting our suffering with Christ. Such a union of love elevates suffering from its natural status as a burden to its grace-filled status as salvific and joyful sacrifice. "Perfect love makes sacrifice a joy."

Therefore, love never flees suffering in fear but transforms it into sacrifice, that is, into a love-offering. Cowards, then, know not love and its power of transformation. They know not the omnipotence of love.

Cynicism

No self-respecting cynic would agree to the omnipotence of love. Love is a feeling: How can mere feelings solve any problems? Besides, they continue, Christ was only speaking metaphorically when he said that the ultimate commandments were to love God above all and to love your neighbor as yourself. After all, how can the emotion of love be obligatory?

If cynics were right in saying that love is only an emotion and if it were also true that no emotion could be controlled, then no one could be obliged to love. But, in fact, emotions can be controlled.[19] And love is not just an emotion. Love, when true, is also an attitude of the will that seeks the good of the beloved. Consequently, any action that seeks to harm someone cannot be an act of love for that person—even if the agent felt lovingly while acting. This means that love requires knowledge —of what is good and what is harmful. And it means that love's duty is to promote the good.

Promote the good? Cynics may still query: Are not love of the good and economic viability mutually exclusive? Ever hear of a moral shark?

Perhaps not, but we have heard of Ivan Boesky, and from him we have learned that even sharks need moral waters to swim in. Without such waters, financial success may not be long lived. But even if it is, its worthlessness is shown by an accurate cost/benefit analysis: What does it profit a man to gain the whole world and lose his soul? (Mt 16:26 and Lk 9:25). Besides, the question at stake here is simply whether the love of the good and its promotion is compatible with economic viability—not whether economic viability can be achieved immorally.

To love others—to promote their good—some have argued, is the very basis of consumer capitalism: an entrepreneur cannot make money without having a product that others find beneficial and desirable. Yet, human nature is fallen: obscene profits earned by satisfying the weakness of others are possible—and beside the point here. It is possible to love and pursue the good while making money. Love of the good does not entail poverty.[20]

But love of the good does entail taking time for relationships, for caring about other people. Yet, in the stress of being successful, we rarely take this time. Douglas LaBier, author of *Modern Madness: The Emotional Fallout of Success*, argues that those who win corporate success often do so by making their careers their top priority. The fallout is emotional maladjustment due to the belief of these "troubled winners" that a successful career brings personal fulfillment. Or I could have cited Dr. Kitchel and characterized these as mistaking their own proper end as also their final end.

This cultural myth has destroyed lives, as individuals substitute love of one's work for love of others. But the myth has yet to be widely seen as the lie it is. Indeed, I'm afraid that its falsity escapes many—for two reasons.

First, atheistic materialism is widespread. And if there is no God, no human soul, then our highest moral activity most likely becomes our work—not individual relationships of love. Why? All humans recognize that one ought to act for the greatest, most perfect good,[21] and most recognize that the self and others equal to the self are neither perfect nor the greatest good. A career unites one to what is bigger than oneself, and this is often identified as being what is greater and more perfect than oneself. Enslavement to one's career or to one's company follows—along with unhappiness. Human happiness requires that loving relationships, and not careers, be given top priority.

Secondly, the myth that careers bring human fulfillment is promoted by a false logic, namely, that since job alienation produces dissatisfaction, removal of alienation would bring satisfaction. However, lack of frustration in a part of one's life does not entail total fulfillment. Human beings are not one-dimensional robots, happiest when successfully turning economic wheels.[22] "Blessed are the poor in spirit, for theirs is the Kingdom of God" (Mt 5:3). Blessed indeed are those who —in trust of the Lord[23]—do not covet careers and material possessions; whose spirits can endure both wealth and poverty with equanimity; whose values give love the highest priority; whose love structures the Kingdom of God; and who heed Christ's warning: No man can serve two masters: God and money (Mt 6:24). For these recognize that human fulfillment requires love and that love cannot be attained without being made one's first priority.

Selfishness

Of all the loves possible to human beings, the one without which none can be happy is the love of what is the greatest good, God. We have already seen that one's career, taken as a god, is a false god; there are others: the state, wealth, pleasure, one's family. But even the pagan Aristotle recognized that such goods are an insufficient ground for happiness. Happiness, Aristotle knew, lies in achieving through our highest action contemplative union with the greatest being, God, the Principle of all motion and goodness, the Unmoved Mover.[24] Aquinas, however, while acknowledging the truthfulness of Aristotle's vision, also acknowledged how tenuous our knowledge of God is in this life.[25] So, even though the happiness of the next life will primarily consist in the vision of God, the happiness of this life primarily consists in the love of God.[26] For in this life, union with God through love is superior to union through knowledge.[27]

Moreover, this love of God, so necessary to human happiness and fulfillment, must be our greatest love. God must be loved above all. Aquinas explains it thus: ". . . every object is lovable in proportion to its goodness",[28] and the greatest good in this world is God, our Creator and our Savior. Loving God above all arises with the awareness of God as this greatest good. And since we are morally obligated to love in accordance with the truth, both Christians and non-Christians are obliged to love God according to their understanding of the greatest being.[29]

Three consequences follow. First, humans are obligated to give priority to the four acts of natural religion that acknowledge God's supremacy,[30] namely, worship, service, prayer, and sacrifice.[31] Secondly, we are obligated to love God more than everything else. This means recognizing that oneself and all other things are subordinated to God and that all should be loved for his sake. Thirdly, one should will that oneself and others be united to God. For, since love always seeks union with what is good (that is why love involves willing that some good be united to oneself or to others), true self-love requires that we will ourselves to be united to God;[32] and true love of others requires that we will others to be united to God. This is the essence of charity: to love ourselves and our neighbor for the sake of God. And, since the goodness of God transcends all other created goods, our willingness to be united to God must be greater than all our other loves.

In short, the commandment to love God above all requires that we be holy. As Mother Teresa points out: "Holiness is not a privilege for some but a duty for all." Holiness is our duty because holiness—in the language of Aquinas—means to be directed to God,[33] to refer everything to him.[34] And this is accomplished through prayer. As Paul says: "Whether you eat or drink, or whatsoever else you do, do all to the glory of God" (1 Cor 10:31).

In modern parlance, such holiness or God-centeredness requires both a cognitive perspective and an affective attitude.[35] The cognitive perspective required must become used to seeing things from the divine perspective,[36] that is, to see every human—even an enemy—as a child of God:[37] "Whatever you do to the least of my brothers you do to me" (Mt 25:40).

Such God-centered love also requires dying to the self and its childish perspective that the self is the world's most important entity.

Dying to the self is a scary thought. And it is one used to justify pitting the natural world against the spiritual world. However, if we remember that in the beginning, "God looked at everything he had made, and he found it very good" (Gen 1:31), we can realize that the "lust of the flesh against the spirit" (Gal 5:17) expresses not the war of the spirit against nature but its war against sin and the self's willingness to sin, i.e., its war against the self that prefers its pleasures to morality. Correcting such a preference is—as Socrates long ago noted[38]— like practicing death, insofar as physical pleasures have no hold on the dead. Moreover, to give up our sins can bring a sadness like death; for we can miss inordinate pleasure and passions. Yet, we must die to this sinful self and become committed to not sinning, i.e., we must commit ourselves to being true to that which God created us to be.

Now an analysis of sin shows that its *modus operandi* is to seduce us into thinking that attaining the forbidden would be "better" than being good. Sin, in preferring a lower good for a higher, is a perversion of love: "For true and rightly ordered love prefers the greater to the lesser good."[39]

Even the ancient Greeks knew that it is immoral to prefer physical and bodily goods, such as food and even health, over spiritual goods such as learning or acquisition of virtue. And, as Aquinas pointed out, it is immoral not to observe the same order in the love of our neighbor that we ought to observe in the love of ourselves. Hence we must desire his welfare in the same manner as we ought to desire our own, i.e., first his spiritual good, secondly his physical prosperity, including in the latter category such good as consists in extrinsic possessions. . . .[40]

Compounding this ancient sin of not prioritizing one's values and actions correctly is our cultural belief that we are not personally responsible for our values. This Skinnerization of our culture fortifies the lazy looking for excuses. The frustration and hatred that inevitably result[41] may erupt in criminal violence that uses fear to achieve power over victims. This urge to power through fear provides feelings of efficacy and thereby helps compensate for the efficacy lost by the refusal to take responsibility for one's own happiness. Yet, the fact that those who refuse to acknowledge their role in choosing their values are frustrated—and possibly in need of psychiatric care[42]—shows that the human psyche was not designed to function passively and in denial of the reality that there are certain goods that we ought to pursue.[43] This is a rejection of our obligation to love ourselves properly by pursuing true goods.

The refusal, born of false pride,[44] to love and pursue the good leads to hatred—often violent hatred—of others. How monstrously hateful egocentric pride can become is shown by the following words of Charles Manson:

> I am only what you made me. I am only a reflection of you. . . . Sometimes I think about giving it back to you; sometimes I think about just jumping on you and letting you shoot me. . . . If I could, I would jerk this microphone off and beat your brains out with it, because that is what you deserve, that is what you deserve. . . . If I could get angry at you, I would try to kill every one of you.[45]

Such hatred is born of the refusal to pursue good and the choice to absorb passively certain values of others. Such hatred reflects a "locking in" of the ego within a prideful self-awareness. In the words of Charles Manson: "When it comes down around your ears, you'd better believe I'll be on top of my thought. I will know what I am doing. I will know *exactly* what I am doing."[46]

Real love, on the other hand, brings a self-forgetfulness that frees one from the confines of self-absorption: altruistic love, as Aquinas notes, is ecstatic.[47] Of course, concentrating on loving Christ frees a Christian ". . . from being so wrapped up in oneself [and one's possessions, anxieties, or whatever] that one cannot reach out to others."[48] Love leaves no room for selfishness.

Thus we have seen that the modern sin of preferring the self and its laziness to reality, while blaming others for one's own problems and sins, leads to hatred of self and others. Indeed, as in the case of Manson, it can even lead to a self-absorption so prideful that the self is held to be God.[49]

Thus, the egomaniac's selfish refusal to love reaches to the heavens. It includes a denial of the self's dependence upon God; and such a denial rejects Christian humility.[50] Moreover, it culminates in a rejection of a God-centered love. For a God-centered love involves an affective attitude that both does not admit ". . . anything into one's heart contrary to Divine love",[51] but seeks his will in all things. Saint Alphonsus de Liguori explains: ". . . perfect love of God means the complete union of our will with God's: 'The principal effect of love is so to unite the wills of those who love each other as to make them will the same things' (St. Denis Areop., *De Div Nom* c4)."[52] Such uniformity brings happiness ". . . because their whole happiness is to fulfill, even in adversity, the will of God."[53] "He who unites his will to God's experiences a full and lasting joy: *full*, because he has what he wants, . . . *lasting* because no one can take his joy from him, since no one can prevent what God wills from happening."[54] In short: "Delight in the Lord and he will give you the desires of your heart" (Ps 37:4).

Sadism, Masochism, and Sadomasochism

But doesn't living according to his will involve being willing to put up with injustice, i.e., being a doormat? After all, Christ did say in Matthew 5:39, "Turn the other cheek."

But this cannot be a command for tolerating injustice: true love involves willing the good, and justice is a good that must be willed. There is no dispensation from justice and its precepts.[55] Indeed, Christ himself did not literally follow this command and "turn his other cheek" in toleration of injustice. In the words of Aquinas:

> But even the perfect do not obey these words literally. Nay, Our Lord Himself when He suffered a blow on the face, did not turn His other cheek. He said, "If I have spoken evil, give testimony of the evil, but if well why strikest thou me?" (John 18:23). Neither did St. Paul, when he was smitten, offer his cheek. He exclaimed, "God shall strike thee, thou whited wall" (Acts 23:3).[56]

Turning the other cheek was not a command for accommodating evil but a command not to have a vengeful spirit,[57] as shown by its context in Matthew 5:38–48. This context uses "turning the other cheek" to exemplify that injustice does not permit a hateful attitude but rather it should summon up greater generosity and love. Christ, who affirms the Old Law's validity, places the law of retribution ("You have heard that it was said, 'An eye for an eye and a tooth for a tooth.' "[Mt 5:38]) within the law of love ("But I say to you, love your enemies, and pray for those who persecute you, that you may be children of your heavenly Father . . ." [Mt 5:44–45]). No longer could the hardness of heart, born of self-righteous anger, be sanctioned by the laws of justice. From now on, the heart must pray for enemies and express merciful love.

Love requires not only praying for our enemies but it also requires—as Aquinas later points out, after citing Proverbs[58]—that we be willing to assist our enemies in cases of emergencies.[59] Such willingness is antithetical to the sadomasochistic passivity of doormats (and antithetical to Dr. Kitchel's spiritual couch potatoes).

These acts of love require a strength of character beyond all doormats. Doormats lack the self-respect and true self-love indispensable for distinguishing between another's evil—and properly hateful[60]—acts and the person who is to be loved.

Furthermore, doormats do not love justice enough to enable them to see that merciful love and forgiveness—rather than belittling justice—are its basis and its fulfillment.[61] Doormats would rather nurse their injuries and dreams of revenge than forgive and move on.

Yet doormats are not alone in this regard: many of us regard forgiveness as antithetical to justice. Louis Evely inquires:

> Through which aberration are we sometimes tempted to prefer [in this life] a regime where God's justice would be like ours, where the wicked would be struck down and everyone treated according to his own worth! Do we not see that this is to wish our own destruction? Where is our chance of salvation? Is it not, precisely, in belonging to an order where the sinners are *forgiven*?[62]

Let us never forget the words of the Our Father: "Forgive us our trespasses as we forgive those who trespass against us" (Mt 6:12). Compassionate forgiveness is central to Christian love. As Ephesians 4:32–5:2 says: "Be kind to one another, compassionate, forgiving one another as God has forgiven you in Christ. So be imitators of God, as beloved children, and live in love as Christ loved us . . ." Such compassionate and forgiving love, modeled on the love of Christ, requires giving up an attitude of self-righteousness that can be highly pleasing —especially to doormats.

But it must be done. Love demands it. Love cannot exist without mercy.[63] Nor can love tolerate the injustice of using and abusing any human being—even if that doormat is oneself. Indeed, Aquinas points out that one is morally obligated to love oneself, i.e., to will one's own good; one cannot surrender personal salvation to save another; evil cannot be done for good. True self-love is so important because it is the basis of altruistic love of others.[64] One cannot pursue the justice required by altruistic love without pursuing it for oneself. Injustice ought never be accommodated.

To pursue justice requires an impartial perspective beyond the sadomasochistic narcissism of most doormats, who prefer contemplating their unjust misery to what is just. Such a preference is against true self-love and true love of others. For love requires pursuing good. Such pursuit cannot be undertaken, without beginning with an appreciation of the self's and the other's unique personhood and the reality of being an end, i.e., an instantiating human dignity. And the pursuit flourishes by focusing on attaining whatever is good for the other. In this way, we not only pursue justice, but we love others as we love ourselves.

Moreover, the doormats' self-absorption in the injustices done to themselves prevent them from truly loving others as they should. For the commandment is "Love thy *neighbor* as thyself." Aquinas explains that this requires prioritizing our altruistic loves so that those closest to us are loved more[65] —according to the matter at hand.[66] The demands of justice increase as the relationships become more nigh. It would, thus, be immoral for parents to feed and clothe another's starving children, while allowing their own to starve and freeze.[67] One's first moral obligations are to one's own: charity begins at home. And charity within the home usually demands the best within us. As Covey writes: "It takes more nobility of character in the form of humility, patience, understanding, and courage to do whatever is necessary to build that one relationship—the family—than to labor diligently and faithfully for the many others outside of it."[68] God, in calling us to love neighbors, is calling us not to an abstract love of humanity (which can be "reconciled" with the destruction of individual lives) but to the more difficult love of individuals beginning with those closest to us.

LOVE: CENTER OF THE CHRISTIAN LIFE 115

Let me stress this point. It is so easy to let familiarity (and the fear of becoming a doormat) blind us to the importance of nurturing those closest to us—through individualized attention, honesty, listening,[69] commitment-keeping, little kindnesses, and courtesies.[70] These acts of love cannot be done unless we understand the individual and make what is important to him as important to us as he is.[71]

Moreover, these acts of altruistic love bring us to life. A songwriter once expressed this central truth in the words: "I learned about life by loving you." This means that the failure to be altruistic is disastrous for oneself and for others. Violations of the "laws of love"[72] encourage violations of the laws of life (cooperation, contribution, self-discipline, and integrity).[73] Yet, our culture tells us that the more involved we are outside of the home, the better we are. But it neglects to tell us that outside involvement cannot be at the expense of those closest to us: ". . . he who does not love his brother whom he has seen, cannot love God whom he has not seen" (1 Jn 4:20). Christians must be more aware of the fact that life's meaning is found in love and not in moving mountains of money or anything else: if I could move mountains, "but do not have love, I am nothing" (1 Cor 13:2).

The love so crucial to Christians is a Christ-centered love that perfects our natural love of those closest to us by elevating our love so that we love them for God's sake and in the divine manner of merciful love. As Covey says: "When we love God and Christ first, we will love our spouse more, not less—with more true love, more wisdom, and more charity."[74] Christ-centered love provides a standard—and power source[75]—for how we ought to love all others and especially those closest to us. For the closest are often the hardest to love because we are so painfully aware of their faults and how little they "deserve" love. But when we see them through God-centered love, we gain perspective: just as Christ did not let our faults, or theirs, dry up his merciful love, we must not harden our hearts against them. We must love mercifully: "I give you a new commandment: love one another. As I have loved you, so you also should love one another" (Jn 13:34).

Does this also mean, as the secularists say (in imitation of this principle of unconditional love), that love is blind? Imitations always fail to convey the full truth. Likewise here. To say unconditional love is blind is to say it ignores the faults of others. But the love of Christ was not so: to his beloved Peter, he said "Get behind me, Satan", for Peter was tempting him away from his mission (Mt 16:22–23). Christ believed not in blindness but in sight: in calling a spade, a spade; or a tempter, "Satan"; or self-righteous Pharisees, whitewashed tombs. Love —as any parent knows—often requires promoting the good by rebuking others for their faults.[76] Love demands truth.

If we focus on mercifully loving others—even enemies—by upholding truth, by forgiving their trespasses, by praying for them, by being willing to help those in need, by caring for the closest the most, we cannot be doormats. Not only will we be too busy; but we will lack the doormat's sadomasochistic focus on the injuries others have done us. Besides, God loves in these ways, and he is no doormat.

Practical Implementation Suggestions

The preceding discussion of how love centers the Christian life raises the practical question of why it is that Christian love characterizes so little of our lives. The answer, I think, is simply that our lives are so busy that we do not take the reflective time necessary for centering our lives upon Christian love—or even for just healthy living.

Now humans, like every living organism, require a feedback mechanism for flourishing.[77] Our best feedback mechanism involves reflecting upon our actions according to evaluative criteria more advanced than the childish criteria of pleasure and pain. This is not to say that pleasure and pain cannot be instructive: all know that when their entire life is filled with emotional pain that something is wrong. Yet, pain and pleasure are not sufficient indicators of what actions ought to be done: if they were, no chocolate lover would have any teeth and all dentists would be extinct. Moreover, the busyness of our lives requires that we *explicitly* adopt a feedback mechanism that enables us to reflect upon whether we are indeed living love-centered lives. The best feedback loop is daily: it begins in the morning with remembering the values and standards we will strive to live up to, and it ends in the evening by reflecting upon how close we came and how we can come closer. For example: Did I respond to my child in a loving way that strengthens his maturity; if not, how can I do so in the future?

The key to this entire process is explicitly adopting as your personal mission to live by the values and standards of your choice. Stephen Covey, author of *The Seven Habits of Highly Effective People*, recommends that every person write a personal mission statement in which you choose how to live out your life's goals according to your values: "It [the mission statement] focuses on what you want to be (character) and to do (contributions and achievements) and on the values or principles upon which being and doing are based."[78] Accordingly, mission statements provide standards for what type of person you want to be; for what things you want to accomplish; and for the values you shall use for actions. Of these three, the values chosen are most important: they determine your character and the goals you deem worthwhile.

Consequently, the statement cannot be written without deepening one's awareness of one's personal identity: for it requires identifying the values, goals, and kind of character one wants to hold most dear. Once adopted, the personal mission statement provides a changeless core of personal identity that enables one to be flexible in dealing with the problems always confronting us,[79] especially those most vexing crosses of close relationships. Indeed, it is too easy in today's hectic pace to fail to do anything for strengthening and maintaining our close relationships: we don't teach our children how to deal with problems, we don't listen to others, we let busyness excuse ignoring important relationships. In short, we lose perspective and forget the immortal words of Socrates: "An unexamined life is not worth living."

Personal mission statements reviewed daily are designed to prevent losing our perspective and our values in the whirl of pressures. This can be invaluable in preventing our succumbing to the terrible cliché that men derive their identity from their work while women derive their identity from their men. Both derivations are prescriptions for unhappiness. For as Plato and Aristotle long ago recognized, happiness lies in virtue, i.e., in doing good and being virtuous. Christ himself requires virtue but with a new twist: he orders us to keep the commandments as an expression of our Christ-centered love (Jn 14:15). Thus, John Paul II writes: "Happiness is being rooted in love."[80] Accordingly, Aquinas argues that love of God brings the greatest happiness in this life. After all, Christ promised to be with those who keep his word through love (Jn 14:23). Consequently, if we can identify ourselves as ones who live up to the standard of Christian love, we can be happy—and grow happier, as our love of God and his children deepen.

Thus, a good mission statement for Christians will not forget that we are already on a mission from God: to abide in his love, to walk in his presence, to do and pursue good, not to waste any suffering by failing to unite it with his redemptive Cross, to love our neighbors his way. Our statements will thus allocate time for praying, for work, and for building and maintaining relationships—especially the closest—through honesty, patience, kindness, generosity, fairness, forgiveness, merciful love, etc. The statement's highest value and priority will be pursuing happiness by loving neighbors as oneself for the sake of God and loving God above all else. In short, the statement will concentrate on living a truly love-centered existence.

NOTES

[1] I wish to thank Dr. Alison Brown and Dr. George Rudebusch for their very helpful comments.

[2] "... Grace perfects nature according to the manner of the nature" (Saint Thomas Aquinas, *Summa Theologiae* [hereinafter referred to as *ST*], I, 62, 5c). Also see I, 60, 5c wherein he writes that charity does not destroy but perfects natural love.

[3] See *ST* I–II, 109, 3c, 4c, 8c.

[4] Pope John Paul II, *Salvifici doloris, On the Christian Meaning of Human Suffering* (Washington, D.C.: United States Catholic Conference, 1984), p. 5.

[5] "First, those who suffer are the true witnesses of the human condition. They proclaim that the world is sick, that human life is impossible. Usually one becomes aware of it only in catastrophes, in those most normal, most foreseeable, most certain events which we call catastrophes. Yes, indeed, in accidents, mourning, illness, war, everybody thinks it obvious that life is too hard, too unjust, too sorrowful, too painful. But our big mistake is not to know it beforehand. The great error in face of an illness, an accident, is to believe that evil is suddenly appearing in an innocent and happy life" (Louis Evely, *Suffering* [Garden City, N.Y.: Doubleday & Co., 1967], p. 65).

[6] In fact, psychologist M. Scott Peck observes that the refusal to undergo legitimate suffering is a cause of psychological problems (*The Road Less Traveled* [New York: Simon & Schuster, 1978], p. 17).

[7] Mary Angelica and Christine Allison, *Mother Angelica's Answers Not Promises* (New York: Pocket Books, 1987), p. 88.

[8] *Salvifici doloris*, p. 39.

[9] "Suffering is in itself an experience of evil. But Christ has made suffering the firmest basis for the definitive good, namely the good of eternal salvation" (John Paul II, *Salvifici doloris*, p. 32). The mystery here is described by Saint Paul in Col 1:24: "... in my flesh I complete what is lacking in Christ's afflictions for the sake of his body, that is, the Church."

[10] Evely, *Suffering*, pp. 28–29.

[11] John Paul II, *Salvifici doloris*, p. 38.

[12] Ibid., p. 33.

[13] In Eden, humans lost the subordination of their minds to God (through their disobedience), their bodies to their minds (hence they were ashamed [Augustine, *City of God*, bk. 13, chap. 13]), and the earth to themselves (hence the earth brings forth thistles, and labor requires sweat [Gen 3:18–19]).

[14] Evely, *Suffering*, p. 45.

[15] Within redemptive suffering "the person can discover himself, his own humanity, his own dignity, his own mission." (John Paul II, *Salvifici doloris*, p. 39). The more a person loves, the greater the rediscovery of the soul thought "lost" in suffering (p. 26).

[16] See also Jer 29:11–12 and Rom 8:28.

[17] An excellent book for giving the divine perspective on the various types of suffering is *Mother Angelica's Answers Not Promises*. One of the many explanations for suffering can be summarized as soul-making, i.e., as opportunities for becoming better Christians. Another is that some suffering is preventive: "This is when God permits a momentary setback or delay or even a painful period in your life because he has down the road something much better in mind" (p. 72).

[18] Evely, *Suffering*, p. 12.

[19] See Nathaniel Branden, *Psychology of Self-Esteem: A New Concept of Man's Psychological Nature* (New York: Bantam Books, 1969), especially pp. 64–78. In these pages, he shows that emotions result from value judgments (that once made can become "automatic"), and so, one can control emotions by controlling the judgments one makes.

[20] Yet poverty may free one to serve the Lord without the distractions that arise from possessions and their care. Hence the vow of poverty in most religious communities.

[21] Aquinas identifies the perfect as man's last end, see *ST*, I–II, q. 1, aa. 5–7.

[22] For an extended discussion against the reductionistic view that human fulfillment and meaning can be found within the work-a-day world, see Josef Pieper, *Leisure: The Basis of Culture* (New York: New American Library, 1964).

[23] "Let your life be free from love of money but be content with what you have, for he has said, 'I will never forsake you or abandon you' " (Heb 13:5). And, "Instead, seek his Kingdom, and these other things will be given you besides" (Lk 12:31).

[24] See Aristotle, *Nicomachean Ethics* bk. 10, chap. 7.

[25] See *ST*, I, 12, 11–12; I–II, 3, 2 ad 4.

[26] The order reverses in heaven because there God will not be known through the limitations of human thought and ideas but as he is in himself. See Saint Thomas Aquinas, *Contra Gentiles* III, chap. 49, n. 7 and chap. 51 and 52.

[27] See *ST*, I–II, 27, 2 ad 2 wherein Aquinas applies to God the claim that ". . . a thing is loved more than it is known; since it can be loved perfectly, even without being perfectly known."

[28] Saint Thomas Aquinas, *The Religious State* (Westminister, Md.: Newman Press, 1950), p. 10.

[29] Aquinas holds both that every human is obliged to love the greatest good the most and that humans have a natural knowledge of God as the principle of good (*Contra Gentiles* III, chap. 38, n. 4). Also see *ST* I, 60, 5 ad 4; and *De Caritate*, a. 2, ad 16.

[30] ". . . it belongs to religion to pay due honor to someone, namely, to God. . . .

(*ST*, II–II, 81, 2c). And, "Again, honor is due to someone under the aspect of excellence: and to God a singular excellence is competent, since he infinitely surpasses all things and exceeds them in every way" (II–II, 81, 4c).

[31] See *ST* II–II, 3 ad 2; II–II, 83, 3c; II–II, 85, 1c; and II–II, 85, 1c.

[32] This is the highest form of altruism: to love God so much as to will oneself to be a gift for him. To be a gift, John Paul II writes, is not only the inner essence of love but it also enables one to discover one's true self. See *Original Unity of Man and Woman: Catechesis on the Book of Genesis* (Boston: Daughters of St. Paul, 1981) and *Love and Responsibility*, trans. H. T. Willetts, (New York: Farrar, Straus & Giroux, 1981).

[33] "That is called holy which is directed to God. . . . For love can only be called holy in so far as it is directed to God" (Aquinas, *The Religious State*, p. 69).

In order to be directed to God, one need not be actively thinking of God at all times: such activity is not necessary because being God-oriented is like walking along a road: in order to walk, one need not actively think of each step (*ST* I–II, I, 6 ad 3). Nor, in this life, is it possible always to be thinking of God.

[34] God-directedness or -centeredness, in this life, is attained by deciding to refer all to God and by detesting sin which withdraws one from God. As Aquinas says: "There is another way in which we love God with our whole heart and soul and strength. We so love Him, if there be nothing in us which is wanting to divine love, that is to say, if there is nothing which we do not, actually or habitually, refer to God. We are given a precept concerning this form of divine love" (*The Religious State*, p. 15).

[35] "Secondly, we love God with our whole mind, when we subject our understanding to Him, believing what has been divinely transmitted to us. . . .

"Thirdly, we love God with our whole soul, when all that we love is loved in God, and when we refer all our affections to the love of Him" (Aquinas, *The Religious State*, pp. 15–16).

[36] "What does it mean to put God and Christ at the center of one's life? The sense of this is seeing our world through the eyes of Christ, with the same kind of perception or map or frame of reference that he has. It is informed admiration and emulation of Jesus Christ, with the intent of reaching for his map, his frame of reference (which of course is identical with that of the other two members of the Godhead)" (Stephen R. Covey, *The Divine Center* [Salt Lake City: Bookcraft, 1982], p. 73).

[37] ". . . for we love them because they are His creatures, made in His image, and capable of enjoying Him" (Aquinas, *The Religious State*, p. 75). Also see Covey, *The Divine Center*, p. 98: "The key is to see others, particularly so-called enemies, as they truly are—children of our Heavenly Father, for whose sins the Savior also atoned as he did for ours."

[38] Plato, *Phaedo*, 67d.
[39] Aquinas, *The Religious State*, p. 69.
[40] Ibid.

⁴¹ George Orwell once observed: "Hatred is inner frustration turned outwards."

⁴² "Those with character disorders refuse to assume responsibility and blame their conflict with the world on the world" (Peck, *Road Less Traveled*, p. 35).

⁴³ The analysis here of the interrelationship between efficacy, happiness, power-hunger, and hatred is taken from Branden, *Psychology of Self-Esteem*. He thinks the key is a refusal to think: "The hatred that such men feel toward other human beings extends ultimately to reality as such, to a universe which does not allow them to have their irrationality and their self-esteem too, a universe which inexorably links irrationality to pain and guilt. To defeat the reality they have never chosen to grasp, to defy reason and logic, to succeed at the irrational, *to get away with it*—which means: to make their will omnipotent —becomes a burning lust, a lust to experience the only sort of 'efficacy' they can project. And since, for social metaphysicians, reality means other people, the goal of their existence becomes to impose their will on others, to compel others to provide them with a universe in which the irrational will work" (p. 189).

⁴⁴ ". . . every sinful act proceeds from inordinate desire for some temporal good. Now the fact that anyone desires a temporal good inordinately, is due to the fact that he loves himself inordinately; . . ." (*ST*, I-II, 77, 5c).

⁴⁵ Vincent Bugliosi with Curt Gentry, *Helter Skelter* (Toronto: Bantam Books, 1974), pp. 526ff.

⁴⁶ Ibid., p. 513.

⁴⁷ *ST*, I-II, 28, 3.

⁴⁸ Joseph Wilson, "Homilies on the Liturgy of the Sundays and Feasts", *Homiletic and Pastoral Review* (August–September, 1990), p. 42.

⁴⁹ Bugliosi, *Helter Skelter*, p. 317.

⁵⁰ Jules Brady, S.J., "Natural Theology and Religious Value", *Homiletic and Pastoral Review*, p. 66

⁵¹ Aquinas, *The Religious State*, p. 75.

⁵² Saint Alphonsus de Ligouri, *Uniformity with God's Will*, trans. Thomas W. Tobin, C.Ss.R., (Rockford, Ill.: Tan Books, 1952), p. 4.

⁵³ Ibid., p. 10.

⁵⁴ Ibid., p. 12.

⁵⁵ See *ST*, I-II, 100, 8c, wherein Aquinas notes that: ". . . any precepts which contain the very preservation of the common good, in the very order of justice and virtue, . . . are indispensable."

⁵⁶ Aquinas, *The Religious State*, p. 99.

⁵⁷ See *ST*, I-II, 108, 3 ad 2.

⁵⁸ "If thy enemy be hungry, give him to eat; if he thirst, give him . . . drink" (Prov 25:21).

⁵⁹ See *ST*, II-II, 83, 8; II-II, 25, 8c; and II-II, 25, 9c.

⁶⁰ Again, see *ST*, II-II, 25, 8c, wherein Aquinas writes it would be perverse

to love that which is evil in another. And see II–II, 25, 8 ad 3: "It is wrong to love one's enemies as such: charity does not do this, . . ."

[61] One cannot love justice without loving the human equality it protects. In the words of Pope John Paul II: ". . . justice is based on love, flows from it and tends towards it" (*Dives in misericordia, On the Mercy of God* [Boston: Daughters of St. Paul, 1980], p. 24).

[62] Evely, *Suffering*, p. 20.

[63] "Believing in this love means *believing in mercy*. For mercy is an indispensable dimension of love; it is as it were love's second name and, at the same time, the specific manner in which love is revealed and effected vis-à-vis the reality of the evil that is in the world, affecting and besieging man, insinuating itself even into his heart and capable of causing him to perish . . ." (John Paul II, *Dives in misericordia*, p. 26).

[64] For a treatment of how altruistic love of self and others is based on natural love, see my "Aquinas's Paradox: From Self-Love to Love of Others", *Proceedings of American Catholic Philosophical Association* (1989), forthcoming.

[65] *ST*, II–II, 44, 8 ad 3.

[66] ". . . we should measure the love of different persons according to the different kinds of union, so that a man is loved more in matters touching that particular union in respect of which he is loved. . . . Wherefore in matters pertaining to nature we should love our kindred most, in matters concerning relations between citizens, we should prefer our fellow-citizens, and on the battlefield our fellow-soldiers" (*ST*, II–II, 26, 8c).

[67] "And who ever does not provide for relatives and especially family members has denied the faith and is worse than an unbeliever" (1 Tim 5:8).

[68] Covey, *The Divine Center*, p. 54.

[69] "True listening, total concentration on the other is always a manifestation of love" (Peck, *Road Less Traveled*, p. 127). Listening is the first step in coming to know others and what would be good for them. Listening is also the primary way in which others receive empathy and feel visible. Visibility is a key ingredient in love, as Branden points out in *The Psychology of Self-Esteem*. For the role of listening in empathy see Stephen R. Covey's *The Seven Habits of Highly Effective People* (New York: Simon and Schuster, 1989), p. 153. Listening requires emotional strength; because, as Covey wrote: "Listening involves patience, openness, and the desire to understand. . . . We find it easier to be closed and to tell and to dictate" (*Spiritual Roots of Human Relations* [Salt Lake City: Deseret Book Company, 1973], p. 8).

[70] Covey, *Seven Habits*, pp. 188, 192.

[71] Ibid., p. 191.

[72] See Covey, *Spiritual Roots*, p. 199.

[73] See Covey, *Seven Habits*, p. 199.

[74] Covey, *The Divine Center*, p. 90.

[75] ". . . They each need a love that doesn't await the 'right' conditions—an

unconditional love. But to show love initially and unconditionally one must have a love supply source which is independent of the human object of that love, one which itself came freely—without request or demand—and unconditionally. For us, Christ alone is that power source. ('We love because he first loved us' [1 Jn 4:19])" (Ibid., p. 88).

[76] Aquinas explains: "Now to do away with anyone's evil is the same as to procure his good; and to procure a person's good is an act of charity, whereby we wish and do our friend well" (*ST*, II-II, 33, 1c).

[77] For a good treatment of feedback mechanisms in one's daily life see Edward E. Ford, *Freedom from Stress* (Scottsdale, Az.: Brandt Publishing, 1989).

[78] Covey, *Seven Habits*, p. 106.

[79] Ibid., p. 108

[80] Pope John Paul II, *Original Unity of Man and Woman: Catechesis on the Book of Genesis* (Boston: Daughters of St. Paul, 1981), p. 122

Laura L. Garcia

FEMININITY AND THE LIFE OF FAITH

Some would say that the status of women in the Catholic Church today differs little from that of the medieval serf, subject to powers from which they are excluded by birth and having no voice in decisions which deeply affect their lives.[1] The traditional exclusion of women from the office of priesthood within the Church is seen as the clearest testimony to this devaluation of women,[2] though the Church's unequivocal teaching on moral issues involving contraception and abortion comes in as further evidence of antifeminine bias. Against this bleak assessment of the status of the Catholic woman today, I wish to argue that women hold an exalted and essential place within the Church and within the wider community of humanity. Women are uniquely gifted, I think, with natural aptitudes for care and concern for others which the grace of God can transform into true Christian charity, the love of others as love of God himself. Women are a sign—in them, the priesthood of all believers finds singular expression and Christ's role as priest is clearly reflected. There is no higher vocation within the Church than to make Christ present in our lives, and no more necessary service to the world.

Scripture teaches that Christ holds a threefold office of prophet, priest, and king, and that all who belong to him participate in this office as well. In his role as priest, Christ offered himself wholly to God as a sacrifice for sin, and we too are called to offer ourselves as "a living sacrifice, holy and acceptable to God" (Rom 12:1). In addition to this role as one who offers a sacrifice, the priest also serves as mediator, acting as God's instrument in bestowing his grace on those who come to him. This suggests two sides of the priestly role: sacrifice and service, a gift of self to God and also to one's neighbor. I believe that women are especially suited to realizing both of these aspects of our universal priesthood and that imaging Christ in this way is the most important service we can perform for the Church.

Let us examine the aspect of sacrifice. We know that our whole vocation as Christians finds voice in the two great commandments: to love God with heart, soul, mind, and strength, and to love our neighbors as ourselves. Love of God consists in offering ourselves completely to him. What God wants from us is not only some of our time or a place within our lives but everything that we are and have. As Mary Hayden points out so well, this call to ultimate sacrifice sounds like the height of folly to the culture around us, but Christ teaches that it is the very opposite of folly: "Whoever wishes to save his life shall lose it; but whoever loses his life for my sake shall find it" (Mt 16:25). Christ invites us to offer ourselves to God completely and unreservedly, as a bride to her Divine Bridegroom, so that we may find ourselves in him.

In his letter on the vocation of women, Pope John Paul II describes this call as a call to holiness, and he points out that the primacy in this order of sanctity belongs to Mary, the Mother of God. In her person, the Church has already attained to the perfection of the Bride of Christ, "having no spot or wrinkle or any such thing; but . . . holy and blameless" (Eph 5:27). The ideal of holiness to which all are called finds its most perfect creaturely expression in a woman. Further, this state of holiness is itself the end toward which the whole hierarchy of the Church is ordered, including the ordained priesthood—its mission on earth is to draw all of mankind into the love of Christ. Far from being excluded from this ministry of the Church, women are called to participate in it fully and to serve as a sign of the self-giving love which is our highest good.[3]

Just as a woman, Mary, stands as a clear and visible sign

of the Church Triumphant, so all women, by reason of their femininity, image in a unique way the character of the Church as the Bride of Christ. This metaphor teaches us that all of us are feminine in relation to God's divine presence, in that, we receive his love in order to return it to him again. Just as with the notion of sacrifice, so too this focus on receptivity as an ideal and as in some way characteristic of femininity grates against our modern sensibilities. But this receptivity to God's love and grace is the only means by which we are enabled to live and act in true freedom, so that, here again, Christian teaching stands our natural reaction on its head. If we as the people of God are to view ourselves as a bride, then it seems that women are privileged to grasp from the inside what, for men, must always remain an acquired understanding. As a Church, we are called to accept with joy and gratitude Christ's gift of himself and to give ourselves completely in return, finding in pleasing him the key to our own happiness. Like Mary, we are called to become Christ's body within the world; to allow him to become incarnate in our lives. When we accept this call, we are but echoing her voice who responded as Bride of the Holy Spirit: "Be it done to me according to your word" (Lk 1:38).

Then, in its second aspect, the priestly ministry mediates God's grace and mercy to his people. Having received the love of God into our hearts, we must allow his love to radiate through us to those entrusted to us. This call to love our neighbors as ourselves cannot be fulfilled unless we have first opened ourselves to the love of God, for, in fact, it is God who loves our neighbors through us, without removing our own freedom or our own essential cooperation with him. Although the virtue of charity requires a deep transformation of our purely natural loves, I believe there are certain qualities natural to women which serve as especially receptive material for this transformation.

According to recent studies, one of the central features distinguishing women from men psychologically is that women seem to value relationships more deeply than do men. In her influential book on women's development, Carol Gilligan contends that while men tend to value autonomy, separation, and individual rights, women place greater emphasis on connection, community, and responsibility. According to Gilligan, "Women not only define themselves in a context of human relationships but also judge themselves in terms of their ability to care."[4] Women see themselves as connected to others by a web of different roles—daughter, sister, friend, wife, mother, employee—and as measured within these roles by the law of love. Gilligan traces the roots of this relational orientation to early childhood development, when boys must separate themselves from their mothers in order to develop a male identity, while girls need not sever this basic connection in finding their identities as females.

Gilligan's thesis concerning the relational orientation of women coheres remarkably well with the Pope's teaching in his recent letter on women. He begins not from the natural factors shaping our identities as women but from the supernatural purposes of the Creator. The Pope explains that since God has entrusted the human being to women in a special way, women by nature seem to possess a deep sensitivity to the intrinsic value of every person.[5] Indeed, one of the clearest pictures we have of the unconditional, unmerited love of Christ for us is the love of a mother for her unborn child. At its best, maternal love desires the good of the beloved for his own sake, without reservation, and at any cost. Further, this kind of maternal love is not limited to those who have children; Mother Teresa comes immediately to mind.

Whatever the source of this natural inclination on the part of women, the placing of relationships and persons at the center of one's life and values serves as a clear reflection of the priorities enjoined by Jesus. Professor Hayden has already emphasized the fact that this ethic of care does not nullify the demands of justice—indeed, there are even responsibilities one bears toward oneself—but it finds a deeper motivation for justice within the love that we bear toward our fellow human beings. Women especially, then, can stand as signs and standard-bearers of the primacy of love, which seeks the good of the other as its own good.

But this is not yet to have reached the priesthood of women, where the goal must be not merely a human and natural love of the other for his own sake, but a divine love of the other for Christ's sake. Our priestly calling requires that we seek above all that Christ may be formed in those around us, just as we labor to admit him into our own lives. In Mother Teresa's image, we are to serve as God's pencils, by which he writes letters of love to each one of his children. The purification and transfiguration of all our natural loves that this requires cannot be achieved without God's grace, and it must also be accompanied by the death of all that is impure or base. In order that we might truly channel God's love to those around us, our natural loves must become modes of divine love. C. S. Lewis eloquently describes this process in his book *The Four Loves*:

> One can see here at once a sort of echo or rhyme or corollary to the Incarnation itself. . . . As Christ is perfect God and perfect Man, the natural loves are called to become perfect Charity and also perfect natural loves. As God becomes Man, "Not by conversion of the Godhead into flesh, but by taking Manhood into God," so here; Charity does not dwindle into merely natural love but natural love is taken up into, made the tuned and obedient instrument of, Love Himself.[6]

When we thus allow our love for our friends and families and fellow believers and fellow pilgrims in this life to be transformed by the love of God, then we mediate to each one the love and the grace of Christ. We make his love present to them and his sacrifice and forgiveness felt by them, because we truly offer them not just our own love, but his. This universal priesthood is surely the highest calling of the Christian, and the most important ministry of any believer, man or woman, within the Church. If as Catholic women we can more and more embody this mission of love within our lives, then we will be faithful servants of the Church; but more importantly, we will fulfill the highest purpose for which we exist: "that we might proclaim the glories of him who called us out of darkness into his marvelous light" (1 Pet 2:9).

NOTES

[1] For example, Mary Daly decries "the perverse consistency in the present trend toward third-class citizenship in the Church" for women in *The Church and the Second Sex* [New York: Harper and Row, 1968], p. 163.

[2] "There will be no genuine equality of men and women in the Church as long as qualified persons are excluded from any ministry by reason of their sex alone" (ibid., p. 155).

[3] Pope John Paul II, *On the Dignity and Vocation of Women*, no. 27 (Boston: Daughters of St. Paul, 1988), pp. 90–92.

[4] Carol Gilligan, *In a Different Voice* (Cambridge, Mass.: Harvard University Press, 1982), p. 17.

[5] John Paul II, *On the Dignity and Vocation of Women*, no. 30.

[6] C. S. Lewis, *The Four Loves* (New York: Harcourt Brace Jovanovich, 1960), p. 184.